CH00731012

Every Christian faces temptati
tempted – Jesus was tempted –
bewildering. Why do we confus
are we vulnerable? Can we win
do we overcome temptation? How do we avoid despair when
we fail? This book by John Stevens addresses these questions
and many more. John combines an astute grasp of Scripture
with an incisive mind and a warm pastoral heart. It is suitable
for Christians at any stage of maturity. As a pastor I would
have loved to have this book in my hands a long time ago. It is
highly recommended.

Paul Mallard
Author of *Invest Your Suffering*
Pastor, Widcombe Baptist Church, Bath, UK

A tremendous study of the anatomy of sin and temptation
in the life of the believer, both biblically and theologically.
Most importantly, *The Fight of Your Life* is replete with ample
resources pastorally to help us where these battles rage most.
A worthy successor to Thomas Brooks' *Precious remedies
against Satan's devices.*

Dave Gobbett
Lead Pastor, Highfields Church, Cardiff
Trustee of Word Alive

THE FIGHT OF YOUR LIFE

FACING & RESISTING TEMPTATION

JOHN STEVENS

CHRISTIAN
FOCUS

Copyright © John Stevens 2019

paperback ISBN: 978-1-5271-0427-3
epub ISBN: 978-1-5271-0498-3
mobi ISBN: 978-1-5271-0499-0

Published in 2019
by
Christian Focus Publications,
Geanies House, Fearn, Tain,
Ross-shire, IV20 1TW,
Great Britain.

Cover design by Pete Barnsley

Printed by Bell & Bain, Glasgow

CONTENTS

Preface 7

Introduction: Redefining the Victorious
Christian Life 9

1. Introduction:
   Is Temptation Sin?..19

2. Explanation:
   Why are we Tempted? 35

3. Theological Foundation:
   Can we Resist Temptation? 67

4. Practical Application:
   How do we Resist Temptation?..95

5. What Should we do when we Sin?....................................135

Epilogue: Rest at Last 157

PREFACE

This book began life as an afternoon seminar track on 'Resisting Temptation' at Word Alive in 2014. It has been honed and developed by the opportunity to preach on Romans and Galatians at City Evangelical Church Birmingham and Christchurch Market Harborough, to teach Galatians in depth on the Midlands Ministry Training Course, and to speak on Romans 6–8 at the St Stephen's and St Wulstan's Selly Oak Church Weekend Away in 2015. I am grateful for all those who engaged with the material on these occasions, and whose encouragement, appreciation and suggestions for improvements have proved invaluable.

The demands of my role with FIEC have meant that I have not been able to complete the book as quickly as I would have liked. I am very grateful for the support of the FIEC Staff and Trust Board, who have encouraged me to press on, and generously enabled me to find time to write. I am thankful to Mike and Judith Dennis, who kindly allowed me to stay in their holiday flat to work on the first draft. I am very grateful to Adrian Reynolds and Laura Dampney, who took the time to read and comment on the manuscript and made numerous helpful suggestions. Helen Jones did a wonderfully efficient job editing my text and correcting the numerous errors resulting from my inadequate typing.

I am especially thankful for the persistence and patience of William MacKenzie in pursuing the completion of this book over several years, for graciously accepting my numerous explanations of why the manuscript had not been delivered on time, and for an excellent family holiday we enjoyed at the Keeper's Cottage at Geanies House in North Scotland. It is a privilege to finally publish this book with Christian Focus.

I am thankful to my wife Ursula and my family for their constant patience and long-suffering, and it is my prayer that Harriet, Oliver, Madeleine and Rosie will discover the liberating grace of the Lord Jesus Christ, and the power of the Holy Spirit, as they seek to fight their good fight against sin and temptation in a culture that is increasingly hostile to the gospel.

INTRODUCTION:

REDEFINING THE VICTORIOUS CHRISTIAN LIFE

The purpose of this book is to help and encourage Christians in their battle against sin, and to ensure that they have right and biblical expectations of the 'normal Christian life'. My concern is that many Christians live with a false burden of guilt and failure, and that they lack hope that they can win the battle against sin in their lives. They have been taught that the battle against temptation is ultimately futile, and that they will never be able to obey and please God. My hope is that they will believe and trust the glorious promises of freedom from sin held out in the gospel because of the death and resurrection of the Lord Jesus Christ, and will appropriate the power of the indwelling Holy Spirit to gain the victory that has been won for them. I want them to know that the 'normal Christian life' is a 'victorious Christian life', and to realize that they are daily enjoying far more victory than they might imagine.

I became a Christian in October 1988 and was privileged to be taught and discipled by faithful evangelical pastors. I was told that the Christian life was a constant battle against sin, and that we have to struggle hard to resist temptation. Whilst there was hope of some progress, it was also taught that failure was inevitable because of the powerful presence of indwelling sin. It was the height of the charismatic movement at that time, and the great enemy of the moment in my conservative circles was an 'over-realized eschatology' that expected too much in the present age ahead of the return of Christ.

In the context of holiness and the Christian life this meant that I was taught to take Romans 7 as a paradigm of normal Christian experience. Whilst I had been justified by faith I was still a 'wretched man' unable to do the good that I wanted to do and beset by sin. The only hope was the eventual resurrection, when I would finally be freed from my 'body of death'. This teaching was contrasted with the Wesleyan model of holiness, filtered though the prism of 'Keswick' teaching, which offered the possibility of 'entire sanctification' and complete deliverance from sin, merely by exercising sufficient faith in the Lord Jesus.

The analogy with the charismatic movement was readily apparent. Both offered the prospect of a second-stage Christian experience beyond conversion that would elevate my Christian life to a wholly new and better level. Our spiritual guides in countering this teaching were men like J. C. Ryle, who wrote his famous book *Holiness* as a rebuttal of the then 'Keswick teaching', and J. I. Packer.

In many ways this teaching was well intentioned as a comfort to those who were struggling with temptation and sin. It brought reassurance that my Christian life was not inadequate and missing something fundamental just because I continued to face a raging conflict with my evil desires. It meant that I was not pointlessly chasing after a 'second blessing' experience but instead focusing on resisting temptation as far as I was able. However, it all too easily provided a justification for my failures to resist temptation and led to a despair that it was even worth trying. Why bother if failure is inevitable? Why does God command me to do what cannot be done?

Alongside this teaching on the nature of the normal Christian life, it was also constantly stressed that we are sinners not just because of the sins we commit, but because of our desires and thoughts. Taking Jesus' teaching in the Sermon on the Mount as a starting point, it was a common feature of evangelistic talks of the era to seek to convict people of sin by drawing attention to our adulterous and murderous thoughts, which deserve condemnation and judgement just as surely as committing adultery and murder.

Whilst it is entirely right to expose the true reality of our sinful nature, which means that we 'sin because we are sinners' rather than that we are 'sinners because we sin', the perhaps unintended consequence of this was to make the struggle against sin primarily a battle not to experience certain thoughts and desires. It created an introspection that was unhealthy. It inevitably led to a permanent burden of guilt and failure. Whilst I might have been able to resist carrying sinful desires into bodily action, I was unable to eliminate them from my mind and emotions altogether. I had no category for separating out temptation and sin.

Whilst I appreciate the solid biblical foundations I received, over time I began to be less satisfied with this understanding of the Christian life, essentially because it failed to fit with what I was reading in Scripture. As I became more conversant with the New Testament epistles it seemed to me that they had a much greater expectation of deliverance from sin in the lives of regenerate believers. I discovered the vital importance of our union with Christ in His death and resurrection, and that believers are a 'new creation'. We are not just justified and declared to be righteous, but also redeemed from the ruling power of sin in our lives.

I had underestimated the New Testament teaching about the power of the indwelling Holy Spirit to empower me to resist sin and win the battle against it. What had seemed the 'obvious' reading of Romans 7 as a description of the 'normal Christian life' because Paul writes in the first person present, as if testifying to his own immediate experience, became less so when I read modern commentaries by thoroughly evangelical authors that highlighted the likelihood of a rhetorical device and the overriding salvation-historical framework of the letter as a whole.

I concluded that I had been warned against an 'over-realized eschatology' but had inadvertently fallen into an 'under-realized escapology'! I had failed to appreciate the extent to which the work of Christ and the Holy Spirit enables believers to escape from the power of sin over our lives.

At heart, the teaching I had received was driven by a pastoral concern to protect against the unreality of a 'holiness teaching' which asserted that it was possible to escape the struggle against sin entirely. Whilst this teaching had been a major issue within evangelicalism in the past, I was not aware of anyone who was actively advocating it, still less claiming to have attained the state of sinless perfection it alleged was possible for believers. The standard teaching was a reaction against a straw-man danger.

I therefore sought to understand the biblical teaching on the normal Christian life, and I have concluded that the New Testament position is different to either of the extremes reflected by the holiness movement and the more traditional puritan approach in which I had been steeped.

The New Testament nowhere teaches that believers will be entirely delivered in this life from the temptation to sin. We remain in our fallen flesh, and until we are resurrected with glorious new bodies we will have to fight against temptation in our lives. There is no 'higher Christian life' this side of the new creation.

However, we are not doomed to a hopeless fight against temptation. The power of sin has been broken by the cross and resurrection, and we are new creatures in Christ. By His power we are enabled to resist temptation and turn from sin. We are enabled to use our bodies to serve righteousness and not wickedness. We can do good and live according to the new desires we have been given by the Holy Spirit. Our temptations are not themselves sin, and we have no cause for guilt when we experience them but resist them. We are not the 'wretched man' of Romans 7, or at least that is not a complete summary of who we are in Christ.

To put it simply, the 'normal Christian life' is not the life described by Paul in Romans 7, but the life described in Romans 8. This is not a life without struggle against sin, but it is a life that offers the hope of victory over sin by the power of the Holy Spirit. We must be ruthless against sinful desires, putting them to death, but we are able to do so because we have been made new in Christ and are indwelt by His Holy Spirit. We fight this battle daily as we look forward to the ultimate renewal of all things.

Rather than living a life of constant failure, we are enabled to live a life of victory over sin. We are empowered to be 'more than conquerors' who stand firm in faith and triumph over all our enemies, including sin. The 'victorious Christian life' needs to be defined biblically. It is not a life of freedom from the presence of sin, sinful desires and temptations. Instead, victory is to face temptations down so that we do not carry them into sinful action. It follows that we are most victorious in the Christian life when we are most strongly tempted and yet put those temptations to death and refuse to yield to them.

Lest anyone be mistaken, the purpose of this book is not at all to lower the standards of holiness required of Christians, nor to offer any easy shortcut way to beating sin in our lives. We are regenerate believers still enfleshed in fallen bodies in a fallen world. The battle will be fierce and lifelong. We are in 'The Fight of our Lives'. However, the victory has already been won, and we have nothing to fear.

My hope is that readers will be encouraged to realize that they can, in the strength of Christ, win the battle against sin, and that this will motivate them to even more determined struggle against temptation. I pray that it will bring comfort, reassurance and thankfulness to God as we realize that we often enjoy far more victory over sin in our lives than we might imagine. Every time we resist temptation and refuse to act on the desire to disobey our Lord, we are living the 'victorious Christian life'.

Over the coming chapters I will set out my thesis and develop the argument, largely through the exposition and synthesis of key biblical passages. I will only refer minimally to the extensive secondary literature that is available. Given that the most substantive treatment of the Christian life in the New Testament is to be found in the book of Romans, much of my attention will be focussed on Paul's teaching in that letter. However, what he says there is echoed in the writings of all the apostles.

Given the need to develop the argument step by step, the applications for our daily lives will largely come in the final two chapters. Once again this follows the characteristic pattern of Paul's writing. Only after we have thoroughly established the groundwork of what God has accomplished for us in Christ, can we begin to consider what it will mean to live this out. I urge readers to read through the chapters in order rather than to leap to the application at the end, as the argument is cumulative and progressive.

Throughout the book I will refer repeatedly to sexual temptation, both heterosexual and homosexual. This is not because I am obsessed with issues of sex and sexuality, nor because I regard other temptations to sin as less serious. It is because the Bible itself repeatedly treats sexual desire as a paradigm model of temptation and uses it to teach the key principles for fighting sin. This is not surprising. Our temptations are 'desires to sin', and the desire for sex outside of the context of heterosexual marriage is one of the most powerful desires we encounter in life. The Old Testament uses the metaphor of sexual desire to explain the temptation of the Israelites to turn from the exclusive worship of the Lord to worship false idols and foreign gods. The power and allure of sexual temptation, and the radical action required to put it to death, makes it a singularly appropriate example to explain the dynamics of temptation and the means of overcoming it. Sadly, in contemporary culture the battle against pornography is one that both male and female Christians have to fight, and one in which many will fail. The somewhat imbalanced use of sexual temptations as a test case in this book is therefore also contextually appropriate and pastorally relevant to virtually every reader.

The first chapter addresses the question of the relationship between temptation and sin, and makes the case that, whilst temptations are desires to sin, they are not themselves sin. It follows that believers are not made guilty before God simply because they experience temptation.

The second chapter examines why Christians still continue to experience temptation after their conversion, and why their temptations as believers may be even stronger than they were before they trusted in Christ. We will see temptation is inevitable because we still live in a fallen world that is under Satan's power and God's judgement.

The third chapter is the heart of the theological argument of the book. It explains how the death and resurrection of Christ has set us free from the ruling power of sin in our lives, so that we can resist temptation and live a life that is pleasing to God. We will see that the victorious Christian life is not a life free from temptation, but a life of resisting sinful desires by the power of the Holy Spirit. This chapter is foundational to the application that follows.

The fourth chapter finally moves to direct personal application and how we can live a life resisting temptation and overcoming sin. This will require dedicated and ruthless action on our part, as we apply the victory that Christ has won for us and enjoy the freedom of the redemption we have in Him.

Finally, the fifth chapter recognizes that Christians do not always win the battle against temptation, with the result that they commit sin. When this happens, we need to trust in the reality of our justification and turn to Christ in repentance and confession to receive mercy, grace and cleansing. The New Testament assures us that God will not cast us away, but rather He will forgive and restore us to close communion with Himself.

My hope and prayer is that this book will spur you to live wholeheartedly for the Lord Jesus, and to fight fiercely and valiantly against sin and temptation. I hope that it will establish realistic expectations for your Christian life and enable you to rejoice in the daily victories you achieve by the power of Christ. I hope it will encourage you to live the 'normal Christian life' of a redeemed sinner, which is so eloquently captured in this recent song from Rend Collective:

> We are more than conquerors, through Christ
> You have overcome this world, this life
> We will not bow to sin or to shame
> We are defiant in Your name
> You are the fire that cannot be tamed
> You are the power in our veins
> Our Lord, our God, our Conqueror.[1]

---

1. Extract from 'More than Conquerors', Rend Collective. Written by Gareth Gilkeson and Christopher Llewellyn, 2014.

1

INTRODUCTION: IS TEMPTATION SIN?

Temptation is not sin; it is the call to battle.
(Frederick P. Wood)

TEMPTATION AND THE CHRISTIAN LIFE

Every Christian experiences temptation. Temptation is best understood as an attraction to sin, the feeling that sinning would be enjoyable and that we should cast off restraint and indulge our desires. The temptations we experience may be fleeting and easily resisted, or they may be deep, persistent and almost overwhelming in their power. Christians long to be set free from temptation because they want to avoid sin and live a life that is pleasing to God and in accordance with His will, as revealed in His Word.[1]

Many Christians feel crippled in their spiritual lives by their temptations. They intuitively feel that the fact that they experience temptations must be a sign of some inadequacy in their Christian faith. Their temptations may cause them

---

1. Romans 12:1-2; 1 Peter 1:2.

to doubt whether they are truly Christians at all, as their struggles against sinful desires seem incompatible with being saved or born again to new life in Christ. They measure their progress in maturity by the degree to which they are afflicted by temptation. They are ashamed of the thoughts and desires that they have, and the power that these desires exert over them. They feel guilty, assume that they are under God's displeasure because of the temptation they have experienced, and long to be set free.

The central question this book will seek to address is whether Christians ought to feel this way about their temptations. Is the fact of being tempted a sign of spiritual immaturity or failure? Ought we to feel guilty before God because we are being tempted, or have been tempted? Is the right and proper response to temptation to confess, repent and seek God's renewed mercy? In essence the issue is the nature of the normal Christian life.

The central contention of this book is that there is a fundamental distinction that needs to be drawn between temptation and sin. All Christians experience temptation, but temptation is not itself sin. The proper response to temptation is resistance rather than repentance. Experiencing temptation does not make us guilty before God and in need of His cleansing mercy and forgiveness. Resisting temptation is the very victory of the Christian life, promised to those who have put their faith and trust in the Lord Jesus Christ and His death and resurrection on their behalf.

The great encouragement of this truth is that most Christians experience a great deal more victory over sin in their lives than they might imagine. Every time they resist a temptation and refuse to act upon it they are experiencing the redeeming power of the blood of Jesus and the mortifying power of the Holy Spirit. They have shown that they are 'more than conquerors through him who loved us.'[2]

Whilst temptation is not itself sin, the temptations that we experience are intrinsically sinful. They take the form either of the desire to do something that is wrong in the eyes of the Holy God, or of the desire to do something that is good for wrong reasons. Our temptations are not morally neutral. But this is not the same as saying that we are morally responsible for them. This book will assert the twin truths that our temptations are sinful, which gives added motivation for resisting them, but that we are not personally guilty of sin unless we choose to act on them. The sinful desires we experience do not automatically make us guilty sinners.

WHY DO WE THINK TEMPTATION IS SIN?

A major reason for the anguish of many Christians, which causes unnecessary doubt and spiritual anxiety, is that we have all too often failed to distinguish between temptation and sin. Far too many Christians confuse temptation, and the desire to sin, with sin itself. The result is that they feel guilty when they do not need to, and they do not appreciate the degree to which they are experiencing victory in the Christian life on a daily basis. Only if we understand the difference between temptation and sin will we be able to appreciate the way in which the Holy Spirit is at work to sanctify us and empower us to resist sin in our lives.

The confusion between temptation and sin has perhaps occurred because some biblical teaching does seem to suggest that temptation is itself sin, and that our feelings are just as culpable and deserving of judgement as the acts

---

2. Romans 8:37.

that we commit. This is especially the case in the Sermon on the Mount, where Jesus taught that true righteousness requires not just external conformity to the law code, but also inner purity of heart and thought.[3] In critiquing the self-righteousness of the Pharisees and teachers of the law, who were the focus of His sustained polemic,[4] Jesus taught that to be angry with a brother or sister was equivalent in the eyes of God to committing murder,[5] and that to look at a woman lustfully was to commit adultery with her in your heart.[6]

It is easy to understand how this teaching might suggest that the temptations we experience are themselves sin, especially when Jesus went on to teach that what makes a person unclean is not what goes into them, but the evil thoughts that come out of their heart, such as 'sexual immorality, theft, murder, adultery, greed, malice, deceit, lewdness, envy, slander, arrogance and folly.'[7]

Jesus' teaching in the Sermon on the Mount is crucially important in revealing the reality of human sinfulness, and for debunking the self-righteous superiority of those who claim that they are acceptable to God because they have kept the law externally.[8] It makes clear that sin extends beyond actions that we might perform with our bodies and includes what we do with our minds and emotions. This was, of course, always the case. Jesus' teaching in the Sermon on the Mount was nothing new, but rather an exposition of the true requirements of the Old Testament law and a correction of the misinterpretations

---

3. Matthew 5:21-30.
4. Matthew 5:20.
5. Matthew 5:21-2.
6. Matthew 5:27-8.
7. Mark 7:20-2.
8. See, for example, Jesus' parable contrasting the self-righteous Pharisee with the repentant tax collector in Luke 18:9-14.

of the Judaism of His day. The Ten Commandments,[9] which are the foundational obligations of the covenant established between God and His people, reach their climax with the final commandment prohibiting coveting:

> You shall not covet your neighbor's house. You shall not covet your neighbor's wife, or his male or female servant, his ox or donkey, or anything that belongs to your neighbor.[10]

In contrast to the other commandments, which appear to prohibit external actions, this command prescribes an internal attitude, namely that of mentally taking for oneself what rightly belong to another. Clearly, what is meant by 'coveting' goes beyond merely finding something that belongs to another person attractive or desirable, or of resenting what another person possesses. Coveting involves imagining taking that desirable person or thing for oneself, and thereby depriving their rightful owner of it and its enjoyment. It is a form of mental theft, driven by jealousy or a sense of frustrated entitlement and injustice. It is an attitude consciously adopted and harboured toward the thing coveted.

Covetousness in fact underlies all the other commandments, since the root cause of the actions prohibited is the preceding desire to take from another what is rightfully theirs. For example, idolatry misappropriates the glory and worship that God alone deserves and gives it to another,[11] murder deprives a person of their rightful God-given life, adultery deprives a spouse of his or her exclusive marital rights, theft deprives a person of their property, and false testimony deprives a person of their life, liberty or reputation.

---

9. Exodus 20:1-17.
10. Exodus 20:17.
11. As, for example, in Romans 1:21-3.

It is not surprising, therefore, that in Romans 7 Paul uses the underlying sin of covetousness as his paradigm example of the way in which the law provokes sin and brings death under the old covenant.[12] Covetousness is universal to humanity and reveals the enslaving power that sin has over fallen human hearts. It is the root sin behind other sins.

In the light of the context and the Old Testament background, Jesus' teaching in the Sermon on the Mount cannot, therefore, be taken to mean that temptation is itself sin. When Jesus speaks of a man looking 'lustfully' at a woman, it does not mean merely that he finds her physically attractive. The language of lust, which is the same root as that of covetousness, is significantly stronger than this, and conveys the idea of a mental imagining of possession and sexual enjoying of the woman he sees.[13] It is illustrated by the mental fantasy obsession that Ammon develops for his sister Tamar,[14] or that grips David's heart when he sees Bathsheba and determines to take her for himself.[15] It is implicit in Jesus' teaching that the lustful look is directed to a woman who is already married, and therefore is not available as a potential marriage partner for the man concerned. Whilst it would be equally wrong for a man to lust after an unmarried woman and mentally imagine her as a prostitute or engaging in extra-marital sex with him, the Old Testament does not condemn a legitimate sexual attraction between those who are available for marriage with each other. This is not lust, in the sense of mentally taking something that belongs to someone else, as is evident, for example, in the Song of Songs.

---

12. Romans 7:7-12.
13. Matthew 5:28.
14. 2 Samuel 13:1-2.
15. 2 Samuel 11:2-3.

In the same way, the anger that constitutes 'murder in the heart' goes beyond mere annoyance with another person and consists in a settled attitude of cursing and rejection that wishes the person were dead, as for example when Cain became angry with his brother Abel.[16]

The point here is not to undermine the deep and real sinfulness of sexual lust, nor of anger in our hearts, but rather to try to ensure that we maintain a proper biblical distinction between desires that remain merely temptations and settled lusts of the heart that are directed towards others and are the equivalent of 'virtual reality' actions in the mind.

THE BIBLE DISTINGUISHES TEMPTATION AND SIN

The reason why it is so important to draw this distinction is because the Bible teaches elsewhere that temptation and sin are distinct categories. Since God's Word cannot contradict itself, we cannot interpret Jesus' teaching in the Sermon on the Mount in such a way as to blur this distinction. To do so not only distorts the clear teaching of Scripture, but also creates significant pastoral difficulties.

The clearest passage that draws a definitive contrast between temptation and sin is found in the letter of James. In James 1:13-15 the apostle is urging Christians to resist temptation and avoid sin:

> When tempted, no one should say, 'God is tempting me.' For God cannot be tempted by evil, nor does he tempt anyone; but each person is tempted when they are dragged away by their own evil desire and enticed. Then, after desire has conceived, it gives birth to sin; and sin when it is full-grown, gives birth to death.

---

16. Genesis 4:1-8.

These verses make clear that there is a step between tempt-ation and sin, which is captured by the metaphor of giving birth. The desire which is evil has the potential to become sin, but this is not inevitable. There is a chain of causation from temptation to desire, desire to sin, and sin to death.

James' purpose in his letter, unlike Jesus' in the Sermon on the Mount, is not to convict his readers of their sinfulness, but rather to urge them never to allow the temptations that they experience as believers to give birth to sin itself. James has already assumed that believers will experience temptations as a part of the normal Christian life, whether arising from the challenges of suffering or persecution in a fallen world that is hostile to them, or from their own fallen humanity.[17] Temptation is a given of Christian experience, but it is not itself the equivalent of sin. His point is that they are to practise spiritual contraception to prevent the desire ever leading to sin, or perhaps even more starkly to abort the desire before it can give birth. The rest of his letter applies this principle to his readers' lives. They are, for example, to resist the desire to show favouritism between their brothers and sisters because of their relative wealth or social status.[18] They are to resist the desires that battle within them so that they do not fight and quarrel with each other. Instead they are to resist the devil and ask God to meet their needs in prayer.[19]

This distinction between temptation and sin is also evident in the original and paradigmatic temptation of Eve in the Garden of Eden. Genesis 3 narrates how Eve was seduced by Satan into eating the fruit of the tree of the knowledge of good and evil, in contravention of the command that the

---

17. James 1:2-4.
18. James 2:1-13.
19. James 4:1-10.

Lord God had given to her husband Adam.[20] As the narrative unfolds, it is clear that there are distinct steps which echo the chain of causation outlined by James in his letter. Eve is first incited to consider the fruit to be attractive and desirable by the lies and distortions of the serpent.[21] Only after temptation has done its work does she take the fruit and eat it.[22]

The key question is this: At what point did Eve fall and commit sin? It seems clear that she only sinned when she in fact ate the fruit, or perhaps at the point at which she lusted after it and coveted it in such a way that meant that eating it was inevitable. The fall was precipitated by her act of disobedience, which was the result of the desire of temptation conceiving and then giving birth to sin. There is no suggestion that she had fallen at the point at which she was first attracted to the fruit and what it seemed to offer her. The fall, with its catastrophic effects for humanity, would not have occurred if she had resisted the desire to eat. The attraction she experienced towards the fruit did not itself render her a sinner under the judgement of God.

Jesus didn't sin when he was tempted

The distinction between temptation and sin itself is supremely revealed in the life and ministry of the Lord Jesus Himself. It is axiomatic to the New Testament that Jesus, the incarnate and enfleshed Son of God,[23] experienced real temptation in His human nature and yet remained without sin.[24] He was only able to make atonement for our sins by remaining sinless, so that He could bear the wrath of God in

---

20. Genesis 2:16-17.
21. Genesis 3:1-5.
22. Genesis 3:6.
23. John 1:14.
24. 1 Peter 2:22, citing Isaiah 53:9.

our place as a substitute and representative.[25] This necessitated Him assuming a true and real human nature, and entering into a fallen world where He would inevitably face temptation. He needed to live a life of perfect righteousness and obedience, which would require Him to face the full force of temptation and yet resist it. As Hebrews 4 verse 15 assures us:

> For we do not have a high priest who is unable to empathize with our weaknesses, but we have one who has been tempted in every way, just as we are – yet he did not sin.

All three Synoptic Gospels record how Jesus was tempted by Satan in the wilderness before He embarked upon His public ministry. Jesus defeated him by resisting his attempts to induce Him to seek the glory of the kingdom without the suffering of the cross.[26] Jesus recapitulated the experience of Adam (and Eve) in the Garden of Eden, and of Israel in the desert, and overcame temptation when they had succumbed to it. Only in this way was He able to serve as the Saviour we need.

The temptation that Jesus experienced was not a mere transitory experience. The way the Gospel writers bracket the whole of His public ministry with reference to His temptations, starting with His confrontation with Satan in the wilderness and ending with His battle against anxiety and foreboding in the Garden of Gethsemane,[27] is intended to convey that the whole of His life and ministry was conducted under the pressure of temptation to rebel against God and take a different path than obedience to His will. In the Garden of Gethsemane He clearly felt the attraction of a salvation that did not require Him to go to the cross and bear the wrath of

---

25. 2 Corinthians 5:21; 1 Peter 2:24.
26. Matthew 4:1-11; Mark 1:12-13; Luke 4:1-13.
27. Matthew 26:36-46; Mark 14:32-42; Luke 22:39-46.

God in our place. There are other occasional moments during His ministry when the reality of this ongoing temptation emerges, as for example when Simon Peter questions His determination to head towards the cross and Jesus rebukes him with the words, 'Get behind me, Satan!'[28]

We have little insight into the inner psychological life of Jesus, but we can rightly assume that the temptations He experienced were deep emotional experiences, in which He felt the attractions of sin and the cost of obedience. This was very clearly the case in the Garden of Gethsemane, where He anticipated the great anguish of the cross and what it would mean for Him to drink the cup of wrath and be separated from the love of His Father for the first time in eternity.[29] Hebrews tells us that He was tempted 'just as we are',[30] so our own experience of temptation is an accurate analogy to His experience in His human nature. The only difference is that we have never felt or experienced temptation with the intensity that He did, because we have never resisted temptation to the uttermost. Only Jesus has been taken to the full limit of temptation and felt its full power.

All too often we discount the reality of the temptations that Jesus suffered. We assume that, because He was not only human but also divine, His temptation was in some sense a virtual temptation that was less than real, and that it was impossible for Him to have succumbed. However, the New Testament will not allow us to settle for such a simplistic understanding. Jesus experienced the attraction of sin and disobedience to God's will, and yet He never lusted in His heart, nor did desire give birth to sin in Him.

---

28. Matthew 16:21-3.
29. Matthew 26:39.
30. Hebrews 4:15.

JESUS AS A PATTERN OF THE NORMAL CHRISTIAN LIFE

Whilst Jesus was unique in His sinless perfection and utter resistance of temptation, the New Testament makes clear that the distinction between temptation and sin that marked His human life will be replicated in our own experience as His disciples. The distinction that James draws in his letter between temptation and sin is spelt out in much greater detail, though different language, by Paul in his epistles, where he outlines the dynamics of the normal Christian life.

We will examine this in much greater detail in the coming chapters, but at this point it is sufficient to note that Paul sees the Christian life as a struggle between the desires of our fallen human flesh and the desires of our new resurrection life in Christ.[31] The Christian is not freed from temptation but is subject to strong and powerful desires that must be resisted and put to death in the power of the Holy Spirit. However, he never suggests that Christians will be freed from these desires ahead of their bodily resurrection when they will be recreated to be like Christ. Once again, we see that these desires are not themselves equivalent to sin, resulting in legitimate guilt and requiring repentance. Rather they are to be overcome, such that they are not carried into action, whether mentally or physically. The proper response to temptation is resistance, but it does not require repentance, confession and forgiveness because it is not itself sin.

THE BIBLICAL UNDERSTANDING OF SIN AND TEMPTATION

When we consider the biblical material as a whole, we find a consistent picture emerging. Temptation and sin are not

---

31. Romans 8:1-13; Galatians 5:13-26.

the same, and we need to ensure that they are kept properly distinct. If this were not the case it would be impossible to maintain the twin truths that Jesus was tempted in every way as we are and yet was without sin, thus undermining the very doctrine of salvation. The apostolic instructions about the normal Christian life would also be incoherent.

The importance of maintaining a distinction between temptation and sin is well illustrated in the context of the contemporary disputes about human sexuality, especially homosexuality and same-sex attraction. Whilst the Bible clearly teaches that sex is God's good gift to be enjoyed exclusively in heterosexual marriage,[32] it is also indisputable that a significant minority of people, including many who profess to be Christians, experience attraction to people of the same sex. Contemporary society views such experiences as evidence of a sexual 'identity' or 'orientation', whether as gay or bisexual, though this is a category that is unknown to the Bible. The question inevitably arises whether people are sinning simply because they experience feelings of attraction to people of the same sex.

Whilst the Bible is clear that engaging in physical sexual activity with a person of the same sex is sinful, as is, by extension of Jesus' teaching in the Sermon on the Mount, lusting after a person of the same sex, there is no grounds to conclude that a person is sinning merely because they experience unwanted and unencouraged attraction towards people of the same sex. Such 'same-sex attraction' properly belongs in the category of temptation and is to be resisted rather than indulged by those who experience it. The desire for a sexual relationship with a person of the same gender is a sinful desire, and not morally

---

32. Genesis 2:20-25; Song of Songs; Mark 10:6-9.

neutral, but a Christian is not rendered a sinner simply because they experience feelings that they fight and refuse to express, whether physically or in mental fantasy.

The experience of Christians who experience same-sex attraction provides a clear and important illustration of the distinction between temptation and sin, which can be applied to many other aspects of life where we feel attracted to disobeying God and His good will for us. Same-sex-attracted Christians who resist lust and sin, by the power of the Spirit, are some of the great heroes of the Christian faith. They are living the victorious Christian life of triumph over sin.

A potential objection to this conclusion that temptation is not itself sin is that the language used to describe these concepts in the New Testament is not consistent. The gospels and letters use terms such as 'temptation' and 'desire' but do not always mean the same thing by them, so that they can be used interchangeably. Sometimes the language of 'desire' can be used as equivalent to 'temptation', as must be the case in Paul's explanation of life in the Spirit in Romans 7 and 8 and Galatians 5. In other places the same word can be used to describe 'lusts' that are intrinsically sinful and equate to what Jesus says in the Sermon on the Mount about sin in the heart. However, this should not be unduly concerning. The New Testament authors were not writing a logically consistent and cross-referenced systematic theology, and the precise meaning of terms needs to be determined in their specific context. It is commonly accepted, for example, that Paul and James used the language of 'justification' in different senses, so that the conflict between them on the doctrine of justification by faith alone is apparent rather than real.[33]

---

33. See for example Douglas Moo, *James,* Pillar New Testament Commentary (Wm. B. Eerdmans Publishing, 2000).

In the same way the language of 'desire' must be considered in the context in which it is used to determine whether it is speaking of temptation or a mental attitude that constitutes sin in itself. Such subtlety in biblical interpretation is essential to do justice to all the biblical texts.

This chapter has sought to establish the basic proposition that temptation is not in itself sin, and that as human beings we all experience an emotional attraction to rebellion and disobedience which is not itself sin. It is, of course, all too easy for this distinction to be twisted into a justification for indulging and enjoying our desires, and for allowing ourselves to enjoy a fantasy life of virtual sin and treating it as of no consequence. However, this very real danger ought not to allow us to throw the baby out with the bathwater and fall into the equal and opposite danger of categorising all temptation as sin. Such confusion will only result in unnecessary guilt, distorted expectations of the normal Christian life, a lack of joy in the deliverance and victory that the gospel brings, and perhaps a resigned acceptance of sin in our lives rather than a vigorous determination to ensure that our temptations are put to death before they give birth to sin.

Whilst temptation is not itself sin, being tempted is the universal experience of all Christians. In the next chapter we will consider why we continue to experience temptation, even though we have been regenerated and united with Christ.

2

EXPLANATION:
WHY ARE WE TEMPTED?

So long as we live in this world we cannot escape suffering and temptation.
(Thomas à Kempis)

Believe that as sure as you are in the way of God, you must meet with temptations.
(John Bunyan)

In the last chapter we saw that temptation is the universal experience of Christians, but that temptation is not itself sin. This distinction does not prevent many Christians from feeling that the fact that they are experiencing temptation must mean that there is something wrong with their spiritual lives. They assume that their faith in Christ ought to bring them freedom from temptation and lessen their struggle against sin. It is vital, therefore, to understand why it is that Christians experience temptation, and why we might experience temptation to an even greater degree after we have trusted Christ than before we became Christians. Only then can we move to consider the extent to which Christians can expect to be delivered from temptation, and how they are to fight to resist temptation in their daily lives.

WE ARE TEMPTED BY SATAN

One assumption that many Christians make is that our temptations are the direct result of the activity of Satan. This is understandable because the Bible clearly narrates the way in which Satan personally tempted both Adam and Eve in the Garden of Eden,[1] and Jesus in the wilderness before He embarked on His public ministry.[2]

There is no doubt that the Bible teaches that Satan is real and personal. He is a fallen angel who has rebelled against God, and his goal is to persuade others to join him in his rebellion. Even though he has been defeated by the death and resurrection of Jesus, he is raging against the church and seeking to cause as much damage and disruption as he can before Jesus returns to judge him and establish His eternal kingdom.[3] Rather like Hitler in the final days of the Third Reich, when the defeat of Germany was inevitable, his goal is to take as many others down with him as he can and wreak a nihilistic and pointless destruction. Paul calls Satan 'the tempter' and worries that he might have persuaded the Christians in Thessalonica to turn away from Christ because of the persecution they have faced.[4]

In both the Garden of Eden, and in the wilderness of the desert, Satan appeared in personal form and engaged in direct dialogue with Eve and Jesus. These narratives reveal the way

1. Genesis 3:1.
2. Matthew 4:1.
3. Revelation 12:17.
4. 1 Thessalonians 3:5.

in which Satan seeks to tempt God's people. His characteristic method is to lie,[5] making God out to be unreasonable and restrictive, and encouraging His people to believe that they can and should throw off His authority and seek their best interests by disobeying Him.

In the Garden of Eden Satan lied to Eve about God's Word, causing her to question what God had said,[6] to doubt God's judgement,[7] and to distrust God's good character.[8] He persuaded her that God's command was petty and restrictive, that she would not die if she ate, and that God did not have her best interests at heart because He was restricting her true potential to become like God. He painted God as a narrow and self-serving tyrant, who did not have the best interests of His creatures at heart. He caused her to doubt God's love towards her and made a persuasive case that the true good life would only be experienced by eating the fruit.

The fruit of the tree of the knowledge of good and evil was a symbol of autonomy from authority, and the assertion of the right to define what is right and wrong for oneself.[9] Rather than seeing this as a dangerous delusion that would destroy the good world that God had prepared for His people, Satan's lies caused her to see the fruit in a totally different way, as a means to self-realisation and fulfilment rather than the path to death and separation from God's presence and His blessings.

Satan's technique was repeated when he tempted Jesus in the desert after His baptism.[10] The thrust of his temptations was to persuade Jesus to seek the glory of the kingdom

---

5. John 8:44; 2 Thessalonians 2:11.
6. Genesis 3:3.
7. Genesis 3:4.
8. Genesis 3:5.
9. 2 Samuel 14:17; 19:35
10. Matthew 4:1-11.

without going the way of the cross. He lied to Jesus about the goodness of God towards Him, and questioned His self-knowledge of His identity as the Son of God. He falsely promised that he would be able to give Jesus all the kingdoms of the world and their splendour, if only Jesus would bow down and worship him.

The technique of Satan to tempt by lying about God and His Word is also highlighted by the different responses of Eve and Jesus to the temptation they encountered. When Eve is tempted in the Garden of Eden, Adam, who had received God's command and was right there with her,[11] failed to intervene and correct Satan's lies with the truth of God's Word. As a result, Eve was deceived, and she failed to resist the temptation and ate the fruit. In contrast when Jesus was tempted in the wilderness, time and again He responded to Satan's lies by quoting Scripture to refute them.[12] The truth of God's Word defused the power of his temptation. It is God's Word that brings a proper perspective on what is right and what is wrong, an understanding of the terrible consequences, both individually and corporately, of disobedience, and which reveals the good and loving character of God and assures us of His ultimate purpose to bless His people.

Whilst Satan was personally active in the temptation of Eve and Jesus, most Christians do not experience the direct temptation of Satan in this way. He does not manifest himself to us in person or address us directly in speech. Unlike God, Satan is not omnipresent, but is limited in his ability to manifest himself to specific individuals. Whilst it

---

11. Genesis 3:6.
12. Matthew 4:1-11, quoting Deuteronomy 8:3; Deuteronomy 6:16 and Deuteronomy 6:13.

is certainly true that Christians find themselves engaged in a spiritual battle against powers of evil,[13] in the main we do not do direct battle against Satan on a personal basis. Satan does not need to tempt us in this way because the lies that he tells have been taken up by the world, which is fallen and hostile to God. Satan has deceived and blinded unbelievers to the truth, and our wider culture has believed the lies that he told about God.[14]

As a result, we are surrounded by individuals and institutions that repeat the lies of Satan and cause us to be tempted to disbelieve God's Word and to disobey His commands. The prevailing message of our politicians, academics, media commentators, artists, novelists and musicians is essentially the same as that of Satan in the Garden of Eden. We are constantly told that God did not really say what we read in the Bible, that there is no eternal judgement to come if we choose to disobey God, and that God's commands are restrictive, oppressive and unjust because they limit our potential for self-realisation and personal enjoyment. Whether it is through pornography, television drama or advertising, the constant refrain is that authentic human existence and true personal fulfilment are to be found in casting off the rule of God and creating our own morality by determining what is right and wrong for ourselves.

The result is that Satan does much of his work of temptation through the wider culture we inhabit. In biblical terminology, the 'world' is not so much a physical and geographical place as an entire system that is in rebellion to God and hostile towards Him. People who belong to the world inevitably exhibit its values and seek to promote

---

13. Ephesians 6:10-20.
14. 2 Corinthians 4:4.

them to us. They are evangelists for sin, whether overtly and aggressively or in much more subtle ways. They can become mouthpieces for Satan, repeating his lies and acting as his propagandist, as for example when Peter rebuked Jesus and urged Him not to go the way of the cross.[15]

Virtually every engagement we have with the unbelieving world thus carries with it temptation to sin, as we are surrounded by its propaganda encouraging rebellion against God and worship of self or others in His place. The apostle John therefore warns Christians:

Do not love the world or anything in the world.[16]

However, it is impossible for Christians to withdraw from the world to avoid temptation,[17] and nor are we meant to do so. Jesus instructed His disciples to be in the world but 'not of the world'.[18] If we seek to separate ourselves from the world, whether in a monastery or a Christian sub-cultural ghetto, we are unable to fulfil our mission. Jesus sends His disciples into the world, as it were, behind enemy lines and into hostile territory, to preach the good news of the gospel and rescue people from their bondage to the lies of Satan and into the kingdom of God.[19] We are called to live out our lives in the sphere of constant satanic temptation, but without succumbing to it.

WE ARE TEMPTED BECAUSE OF OUR FALLEN FLESH

Don't excuse yourself by accusing Satan. (Thomas Brooks)

---

15. Mark 8:32-33.
16. 1 John 2:15.
17. 1 Corinthians 5:10.
18. John 17:15-16.
19. Acts 26:18; Colossians 1:13.

Whilst temptation certainly originated with Satan, and he is active in tempting Christians through the lies that have now become embedded in the world and its culture, it is a mistake to think that the problem of temptation for Christians is primarily external. Whilst the individuals and institutions we encounter may well cause us to be tempted, the primary source of temptation lies in our own selves. We are subject to a constant bombardment of temptation that comes from within. This means that we cannot ultimately escape temptation by separating ourselves from the wider world, or by seeking to live in a solely Christian sub-culture. Those who seek deliverance in this way will quickly discover that they have taken the problem of temptation with them, since it is part of their very being.

The frustration that many Christians feel in their spiritual lives because of the persistent ferocity of the battle they face against temptation can only begin to be overcome if they gain a proper biblical understanding of their own existence and experience. The battle against sin is essentially a battle within and against themselves, that they must fight by the power of the Spirit on the basis of the victory that Christ has won for them on the cross.

Human beings were created by God in His image in original righteousness.[20] As such Adam and Eve in the Garden experienced no temptation from within themselves. They willingly accepted God's good rule and would have had no thought of disobeying His command not to eat from the tree of the knowledge of good and evil. They would not have felt any element of attraction towards the idea of eating it. Their rebellion required an external tempter to cast doubt

---

20. Genesis 1:26-7.

in their minds and put the idea of rebellion in their heads. It took Satan and his lies to cause them to feel that it would be desirable to eat the fruit and obtain what he had falsely promised that it would bring.

In the same way Jesus, as the last Adam[21] and the perfect image of God,[22] did not experience internal temptation. His incarnate humanity was in the form of sinful man,[23] but He was not born with the taint of original sin.[24] He had to be tempted from the outside, as He was by Satan in the wilderness[25] and by Peter on the roads around Caesarea Philippi.[26]

The experience of Adam and Eve in the Garden of Eden was thus unique, because their primordial rebellion, and the judgement of God upon it, changed the situation of humanity forever. Whilst the image of God was not erased from humanity, the image was marred by their rebellion and the status of original righteousness was lost. As Paul explains in his letter to the Romans, the judgement of God on this original sin extended beyond their exile from the Garden and the onset of frail mortality.[27] God 'gave them over' to sin, with the result that their hearts were now ruled by sinful desires, including sexual lusts and same-sex attraction.[28] Paul makes clear that sin is not just wrong things that we do, but is personified as a master who rules over us.[29]

In summary, human beings have been condemned by God to the rule of sin in their lives, such that they have a

---

21. 1 Corinthians 15:45-48.
22. Colossians 1:15; Hebrews 1:3.
23. Romans 8:3.
24. As indicated by His virgin birth: Matthew 1:18-25; Luke 1:26-38.
25. Matthew 4:1-11.
26. Mark 8:27-33.
27. Genesis 3:22-24.
28. Romans 1:18-32.
29. Romans 6:14.

'sin-orientation' which manifests itself in attraction to sin. The result is that we became self-tempters, with hearts that constantly urge us to disobedience and wickedness. This is the state of original sin that has been inherited by every human being since Adam.[30] We are born into guilt, condemnation, death and bondage to sin. By ourselves we are unable to resist these temptations, so the ruling power of sin in our lives causes us to commit sins. In the language of James, the desires we experience because we have been handed over by God to sin inevitably conceive and give birth to sin which, when it is full grown, gives birth to death.[31]

The Old Testament consistently and repeatedly describes this fallen state of humanity and our bondage to internal temptation. Our hearts, by which is meant the 'decision-making centre of our personality', encompassing our thoughts, will and emotions, have become wicked and corrupt. Both before and after the flood God's verdict on humanity was that 'every inclination of the human heart is evil from childhood.'[32] Although God rescued His people from their slavery in Egypt and gave them His good and holy Law at Mount Sinai,[33] they were unable to keep it because their hearts had not been changed. They repeatedly fell into gross and wicked idolatry and worshipped the false and demonic gods of the other nations because they were unable to love Him with all their heart, mind, soul and strength.[34] God also revealed the fundamental problem of their hearts through the prophets, as for example in Jeremiah 17 verse 9 where He says:

---

30. Romans 5:12.
31. James 1:14-15.
32. Genesis 8:21 and also Genesis 6:5.
33. Exodus 19-20.
34. Deuteronomy 6:5.

The heart is deceitful above all things
and beyond cure.
Who can understand it?

Jesus Himself pronounced a similarly damning verdict on humanity in His teaching. He repeatedly denounced the hypocrisy of mere external law-keeping, and exposed the true heart-problem that afflicted even the most zealous Jews of the day. In Mark 7:18-23 He berated His disciples for their failure to understand that true purity was not a matter of food and ritual purity but of the heart:

> Are you so dull? ... Don't you see that nothing that enters a person from the outside can defile them? For it doesn't go into their heart but into their stomach, and then out of the body... What comes out of a person is what defiles them. For it is from within, out of a person's heart, that evil thoughts come – sexual immorality, theft, murder, adultery, greed, malice, deceit, lewdness, envy, slander, arrogance and folly. All these evils come from inside and defile a person.[35]

This teaching reflects the true nature of those who are not regenerate Christians with living faith in Christ. They have been given over to the ruling power of sin by God, and their hearts are corrupt and constantly tempting them to sin. They have no power to resist these temptations. They are sin-addicts who are enslaved to their desires. This is exactly how Paul describes the condition of unbelievers in his letter to the Ephesians, as he reminds Christians what they were like before they came to faith and new life in Christ:

> As for you, you were dead in your transgressions and sins, in which you used to live when you followed the ways of this

---

35. Mark 7:18-23.

world and of the ruler of the kingdom of the air, the spirit who is now at work in those who are disobedient. All of us also lived among them at one time, gratifying the cravings of our flesh and following its desires and thoughts. Like the rest we were by nature deserving of wrath.[36]

The fallen nature of humanity, corruption of the human heart and inability of the law to address the problem, required God to deal with this fundamental heart-problem. He could not just forgive His people for their sins but needed to deliver them from their bondage to sin. He promised that He would make a 'new covenant' with His people, which would be different to the old Mosaic covenant of the Law entered at Mount Sinai, and that He would give them new hearts that were free from this sin-orientation.

Jeremiah looked ahead to a day when God would restore His people, who were currently under judgement and facing exile in Babylon, and make a new covenant with them:

> I will put my law in their minds
> and write it on their hearts.
> I will be their God
> and they will be my people.[37]

Ezekiel similarly looked forward to a day when God would 'resurrect' His dead people in exile, and transform their hearts so that they would no longer turn to worship idols:

> I will sprinkle clean water on you, and you will be clean; I will cleanse you from all your impurities and from all your idols. I will give you a new heart and put a new spirit in you; I will remove from you your heart of stone and give you a

---

36. Ephesians 2:1-3.
37. Jeremiah 31:33.

heart of flesh. And I will put my Spirit in you and move you to follow my decrees and be careful to keep my laws.[38]

The nexus of promises associated with the new covenant, in these passages and others, thus includes the definitive and full forgiveness of sins, the provision of a new heart that is inclined to obey God rather than to rebel against Him, and the gift of God's own presence by His Spirit in the lives of His people, to motivate and empower them to live in obedience to His commands. Put more simply, the new covenant will have the effect that God's people are no longer tempted because they have fallen, corrupt hearts, and they are enabled to resist temptation because they are indwelt by His Spirit.

The great news for Christians is that Jesus has now fulfilled the promises of the prophets, and the new covenant has been inaugurated by His death, resurrection and ascension to glory. Jesus Himself made clear at the Last Supper that His death would inaugurate the new covenant. The cup He commanded to be drunk in future at the Lord's Supper, symbolising His sacrificial death and the cleansing atonement made by His blood, was introduced with the words:

This cup is the new covenant in my blood, which is poured out for you.[39]

Jesus' death and resurrection have dealt definitely with sin and removed the guilt and condemnation of those who put their trust in Him. Following His ascension, on the day of Pentecost He poured out His Spirit on His people,[40] with the result that the Holy Spirit was no longer given to empower a few people

---

38. Ezekiel 36:25-7. See also Ezekiel 11:18-20 where God makes almost identical promises.
39. Luke 22:20.
40. Acts 2:1-13.

for special service but would indwell all of God's people permanently.[41] This once-for-all outpouring of the Spirit ushered in the 'last days', the final period of salvation history before Jesus returns to establish His kingdom on earth.[42]

The letter to the Hebrews makes crystal clear that this new covenant has now been established by Jesus, with the result that Jewish-background Christians should not return to the obsolete rituals of the old covenant, as they were merely shadows that pointed ahead to the greater reality that has come in Christ.[43] Paul likewise saw his gospel ministry in the power of the Spirit as more glorious and effective than the ministry of the law under the old covenant,[44] and explained at length in Galatians how the new creation has come in Christ, who had fulfilled the promises made to Abraham by the gift of the Spirit, thus rendering the law obsolete because it had fulfilled its purpose of leading God's people to faith in Christ.[45] In a similar vein the prologue of John's Gospel proclaims that the Old Testament promises of a new covenant have been fulfilled in Jesus. Whereas the law was given through Moses, 'grace and truth came through Jesus Christ.'[46] The signs that Jesus performed in the course of His ministry were foretastes of the new creation, and He repeatedly anticipated the gift of the Spirit to His disciples after His resurrection and ascension to enable them to accomplish their mission.[47]

The consequence is, therefore, that Christians are in a totally different situation to those who are unbelievers, or even

---

41. Acts 2:17; Romans 8:9; Galatians 3:2; Ephesians 1:13-14.
42. Acts 2:16-21.
43. Hebrews 8:1-13.
44. 2 Corinthians 3:7-18.
45. Galatians 3:1-4, 7.
46. John 1:17.
47. John 14:13-31; 15:26-16:15; 20:19-23.

to those who lived under the old covenant in anticipation of the coming of Christ. People who put their faith and trust in Christ are not merely forgiven their sins, but they are also recreated and remade. They have been given new hearts that are now inclined to obey God and are indwelt by the Spirit of God. To become a Christian is to be regenerated, born-again, renewed or recreated. We are no longer what we were. As Paul puts it in 2 Corinthians 5 verse 17:

> Therefore, if anyone is in Christ, the new creation has come: the old has gone, the new is here!

Christians are therefore no longer people who have hearts that are uniformly inclined to evil, nor are their hearts deceitful above all things in the way that they once were. Paul's whole point in Ephesians 2, which was cited above, is that the Christians he was addressing were not what they had been. They were no longer spiritually dead in their trespasses and sins, following the ways of Satan and their sinful cravings. They had been resurrected with Christ, are being restored into the image of God and are living a new life of love and mutual submission. This is true for all those who have been included in Christ by believing the message of the gospel.[48]

There is therefore a very real sense in which the temptations that afflict a regenerate Christian because of their fallen flesh are external rather than internal. Their identity is now found in Christ. They are a new creation and a new person in Him. They have a new heart. Their flesh is no longer their true self, but an alien entity from which they have been separated by death with Christ. As Paul puts it in Galatians 2 verse 20:

---

48. Ephesians 1:13.

> I have been crucified with Christ and I no longer live, but Christ lives in me. The life I live in the body, I live by faith in the Son of God, who loved me and gave himself for me.

This distinction between the old self and the new self, the new creation and the fallen flesh, is what makes it possible for the Christian to experience the temptation of sinful desires but not to thereby sin. The desires of my flesh are no longer my desires in the way that they were before I became a new creation in Christ. My new self is not responsible for them, nor is it morally accountable for them if I resist them and refuse to act on them.

It follows that it is a fundamental categorical mistake to assume that Christians experience internal temptation in just the same way as those who are unbelievers. This is to downplay, or to doubt, what the Word of God clearly says, and to underestimate the transformative impact of our conversion and regeneration. It is to lose sight of the scale of the victory that Christ has won for us, and the reality of our transfer from the kingdom of Satan into the kingdom of the beloved Son of God[49] and of our new life and identity in Christ.

However, the fact that Christians have been regenerated and received new hearts does not mean that they are no longer subject to temptation. The new covenant has been inaugurated, but it has not yet been consummated. Christians live in an overlap of the ages, simultaneously experiencing life in this present evil age[50] and at the same time the life of the age to come. They experience both a 'now' and a 'not yet' of salvation. They are saved, and yet they are awaiting the fullness of salvation when Jesus returns. They have been

---

49. Colossians 1:13.
50. Galatians 1:4.

spiritually resurrected from death,[51] and yet their bodies are still mortal and will experience physical death. They have been redeemed, and yet are still awaiting the full redemption of their bodies. They are new creations, and yet they are waiting patiently for the return of Jesus, the final judgement and the renewal of the whole cosmos when the creation will be liberated from its frustration and bondage to decay.[52]

During this final period of salvation history, Christians find themselves in the situation of having renewed and regenerate hearts, indwelt by the Holy Spirit, but still embodied in fallen human flesh and living in a fallen hostile world in rebellion to God. This biblical balance is crucial to understanding the normal Christian life, and our experience of ongoing internal temptation.

The apostle Paul wrestles with these issues more than any other New Testament author, as he sets out his gospel and explains how Christ has brought both forgiveness and freedom from sin. He wants to guard both the wonderful truth that Christians have been set free from sin, because the new covenant has been inaugurated, but at the same time to explain that the Christian life is a permanent battle against sin and temptation. Paul's teaching leaves no place for those who would say that the Christian life is a hopeless battle against temptation that we are always destined to lose, nor for those who would claim that the work of Christ and the power of the Spirit can so liberate us from sin that we no longer experience any temptation at all. He will permit neither an over-realized, nor an under-realized, redemption and sanctification. Paul's understanding of salvation and anthropology leaves no room for a complacent despair that justifies and excuses our failure

---

51. Ephesians 2:5.
52. Romans 8:18-25.

to resist temptation, nor a confident perfectionism which denies the ongoing presence of sin and temptation.

Paul describes the nature of the normal Christian life most clearly in his letters to the Galatians and Romans, where he is grappling with the issue of the role of the law in the Christian life. His primary point is that Christians do not, and indeed cannot, live by the law, but are to live in the new way of the Spirit.[53] In the course of his argument he explains that the law is incapable of dealing with the problem of the sinful desires that we experience, which are produced by our fallen human flesh.

In Galatians Paul characterizes the Christian life as a conflict between two competing sets of desires that we experience. On the one hand we experience the desires of the flesh, by which he means our fallen humanity. These are in conflict with the desires that are generated by the indwelling presence of the Holy Spirit. Paul writes:

> So I say, walk by the Spirit, and you will not gratify the desires of the flesh. For the flesh desires what is contrary to the Spirit, and the Spirit what is contrary to the flesh. They are in conflict with each other, so that you do not do whatever you want. But if you are led by the Spirit, you are not under the law.[54]

Paul clearly teaches that Christians will experience competing and conflicting desires. The normal Christian life requires believers to decide which of these desires will prevail and determine their actions. If the desires of the flesh win out, believers will commit the 'acts of the flesh', which include:

---

53. Romans 7:1-6; Galatians 5:13-26.
54. Galatians 5:16.

> ... sexual immorality, impurity and debauchery; idolatry
> and witchcraft; hatred, discord, jealousy, fits of rage, selfish
> ambition, dissensions, factions and envy; drunkenness,
> orgies and the like.[55]

However, if they live by the Spirit they will refuse to indulge
these desires of the flesh, and will instead produce and exhibit
the fruit of the Spirit – love, joy, peace, forbearance, kindness,
goodness, faithfulness, gentleness and self-control – in their
transformed community relationships.[56]

Paul's point is not that Christians, who have the Spirit
dwelling within them, are freed from the battle against
temptation, but rather that they are enabled to resist the
temptations that arise from their fallen human flesh. In the
context of Galatians, his assertion that those who live by the
Spirit 'do not do what you want' most likely means that they
do not act to gratify the desires of the flesh but rather resist
them.[57] Whilst the language seems very similar to that of
Romans 7 verse 19, where it describes a person's yielding to
temptation, the flow of the argument in Galatians suggests
that it means exactly the opposite there.

Paul makes an identical argument in Romans 8. Once
again, he emphasizes how Christians are to live by the Spirit
rather than the law, and explains that they face a conflict
between the desires of the flesh and the desires of the Spirit.
They have to decide which of these competing sets of desires
will rule over them and determine their actions:

> Those who live according to the flesh have their minds set
> on what the flesh desires; but those who live in accordance

---

55. Galatians 5:19-21.
56. Galatians 5:22-23.
57. See for example Thomas Schreiner, *Galatians* Exegetical Commentary on the
New Testament (Zondervan, 2010).

with the Spirit have their minds set on what the Sprit desires. The mind governed by the flesh is death, but the mind governed by the Spirit is life and peace. The mind governed by the flesh is hostile to God; it does not submit to God's law, nor can it do so. Those who are in the realm of the flesh cannot please God.[58]

Paul's whole point is that Christians, who have been regenerated and are indwelt by the Holy Spirit, no longer live in the realm of the flesh but in the realm of the Spirit, and are therefore able to resist the desires of the flesh.[59] However this will always be a battle they must fight, and the crucial thing is that they fight it in the right way.

Paul's teaching in Galatians and Romans teases out the radical difference between life under the old covenant of the law and under the new covenant that has been established by Christ. Christians still continue to experience internal temptation, and to be racked by sinful desires, but these have a different source and they are counterbalanced by the new desires that come from the indwelling presence of the Spirit.

Notably and significantly, Paul does not describe Christians as having a corrupt heart as the seat of the desires that tempt them to sin. As has been mentioned above, in the Bible the heart encompasses not only the emotions but also what we would term the mind and the will. As far as Paul is concerned Christians now have renewed minds,[60] which are able to approve God's good, pleasing and perfect will, and they are therefore able to fulfil the obligations of love set out in the law.[61]

---

58. Romans 8:5-8.
59. Romans 8:9-13.
60. Romans 12:1-2
61. Romans 13:8-10; cf. also 2:14-15.

This is a far cry from the total depravity of the fallen human heart as described in the Old Testament. Paul instead sees the source of our sinful desires as our 'flesh'. This term does not simply mean our physical bodies, as if they in themselves were evil rather than part of God's good creation, but rather our fallen human nature which has been inherited from Adam. This fallen humanity is inevitably bound up with our current physical bodies, which were conceived in original sin. Some Bible translations have therefore rendered the relevant term as 'sinful nature' rather than 'flesh' so as to capture this sense. We will remain in our fallen human flesh until we die. Only then will we be separated from it and ultimately resurrected in a glorious and renewed 'spiritual' body like the resurrection body of the Lord Jesus.[62] Then we will no longer experience any sinful desires and will be utterly free from the battle against temptation.

In summary, the New Testament tells us that, as a result of our faith in Christ and the regenerating work of the Holy Spirit, we have been given new hearts, but that we continue to exist in our fallen human flesh. This creates the felt experience of temptation and struggle, as the desires of our flesh compete with the desires of the Spirit. This struggle will continue for as long as we live 'in the body' and have not gone to be with the Lord.[63] Nothing less than death will set us free from the battle against temptation, and our ultimate eternal freedom from sin will be brought about by our physical resurrection when Jesus returns. It is no wonder that Paul longs to be delivered from his fallen human body, which he characterizes as 'this body that is subject to death'.[64]

---

62. 1 Corinthians 15:42-49.
63. 2 Corinthians 5:1-10.
64. Romans 7:24.

However, this struggle is emphatically not the same as the struggle we experienced before we trusted in Christ, and that those who are not yet regenerate experience. We live after the inauguration of the new covenant, and we have received new hearts and the Spirit. Our struggle against temptation is just as real and fierce, but it is not the hopeless struggle that we faced when we were outside of Christ and did not have the indwelling help of the Holy Spirit.

> Let no man think himself to be holy because he is not tempted, for the holiest and highest in life have the most temptations. How much higher the hill is, so much is the wind there greater; so, how much higher the life is, so much the stronger the temptation of the enemy. (John Wycliffe)

Experientially this struggle against temptation may feel harder than it did before we believed, and we will certainly be more conscious of our failures and sins. This is to be expected. Prior to our regeneration we were not aware of the full extent of our sinfulness, just as Paul was not aware of the inadequacy of his pre-conversion law-keeping.[65] We were not resisting sin with full vigour out of a desire to honour God and please Him, but because of a sinful legalism that sought to establish our own righteousness, or out of a desire to achieve some level of social conformity or respectability by adherence to an external code of behaviour. Now that we are resisting temptation in the right way, and for the right reasons, it is not surprising that the battle has become more intense. The enemy has to fight back against our new desires and resolve. The growing ferocity and intensity of the struggle is therefore more likely to be evidence of the progress that we are making in our spiritual walk rather than of our failure and immaturity.

---

65. Philippians 3:6-7.

WE ARE USUALLY TEMPTED BY A COMBINATION OF INTERNAL AND EXTERNAL FACTORS

As we have seen, the temptations that we experience may be a result of the lying activity of Satan, whether directly or indirectly through the false beliefs that are propagated by our culture, or of the internal desires that are a result of our fallen human flesh, which became corrupt at the Fall and was handed over by God to the ruling power of sin.

In reality, the experience of temptation usually involves a combination of these elements. We are tempted by external stimuli, which feed the sinful desires that flow from our fallen human flesh. Our resolve to resist is then diminished by the Satanic lies that we encounter, which seek to persuade us that an action or attitude would not be sin, or that indulging in it would not have any consequences. This potent combination makes the thought of sinning attractive and cost-free and holds out the promise of fulfilment and happiness if only we indulge our desires.

The combination of our corrupted sinful desires, and the Satan-inspired lies about sin, has the effect that we are even tempted by the good things of God's creation. We desire to use and misuse them to establish our own identity and pleasure rather than to receive them as the good gifts that He has given. The characteristic temptations that we face involve the misuse of sex, money and power, idolising and worshipping created things[66] in place of the one true God who has revealed Himself in His Word and supremely in Jesus Christ. We are gripped by 'the lust of the flesh, the lust of the eyes, and the pride of life'[67] so that things which are innocent in themselves become

---

66. Romans 1:25; Ephesians 5:5; 2 Timothy 3:1-5. See especially Tim Keller, *Counterfeit Gods*.
67. 1 John 2:16.

snares to us, because we want what we are not entitled to have, we want an excess of what we are entitled to have, or we want what we are entitled to have for the wrong motives.

Food, sex, possessions, money, security and even authority are not bad things in themselves but are part of the good world created by God.[68] However they can become temptations to us because we view them in a twisted way. They are to be enjoyed only within the boundaries that God has set for them. Food and wine, for example, are good gifts in themselves, but they can easily become the source of temptation to overindulgence, through greed and drunkenness.

This interaction between external and internal factors is seen in multiple biblical examples where God's people succumbed to temptation. It was clearly operative when David committed adultery with Bathsheba.[69] David happened to catch a glimpse of a beautiful woman bathing when he was walking on his roof. The naked human body is not inherently evil, but seeing a beautiful woman was a stimulus to the lustful desires of his fallen flesh. The good thing that God had created became a temptation to him. His decision to abuse his authority as king and send for her, so that he could use her sexually, was presumably influenced by Satanic lies that he was entitled to take what he wanted, that God had withheld this pleasure from him, and that he would be able to get away with it because her husband was away fighting at the front line. This combination of elements led him to 'despise the word of the LORD by doing what is evil.'[70]

The lustful desires of our flesh may be stirred and inflamed by the mere sight of perfectly innocent aspects of God's good

---

68. 1 Timothy 4:4-5.
69. 2 Samuel 11:1-4.
70. 2 Samuel 12:9.

creation. David caught a glimpse of Bathsheba when she was washing, and there is no suggestion that she was seeking to attract him or to seduce him. However, God's good gifts can be offered and displayed in ways that are deliberately tempting and calculated to inflame the sinful desires of our fallen flesh. The prostitute or adulteress dresses in a deliberately provocative way to inflame the lust of those who see her.[71] Her modern equivalent is pornographic imagery, which is intended to incite lust, leading to virtual fornication or masturbatory fantasies. The majority of advertising is carefully designed to stimulate lust for possessions and experiences, promoting them as a way of achieving fulfilment, happiness, identity or of gaining superiority over others. Things that are good in themselves are packaged in a way that is intended to prompt sinful discontent, dissatisfaction and desire, with the goal of persuading people that they need to acquire what is being promoted.

As we will see in subsequent chapters, resisting temptation will require us to confront all these dimensions of the attraction of sin, including repressing the sinful desires of our flesh, rejecting the Satanic lies that encourage us to sin, and avoiding the external stimuli that inflame the desires of our flesh and give opportunity for sin.

WE ARE NOT TEMPTED BY GOD

God never tempts any man. That is Satan's job.[72]
(Billy Graham)

The temptations that we experience as Christians derive primarily from of our own fallen flesh, compounded by the lies of Satan that are deeply embedded in the culture of the

---

71. As for example in Proverbs 7:10-27.
72. Blanchard, John; *The Complete Gathered Gold*, p. 630.

world. However, the New Testament assures us that they do not derive from God Himself. James makes this clear in his letter, where he says:

> When tempted, no one should say, 'God is tempting me.' For God cannot be tempted by evil, nor does he tempt anyone.[73]

As we have already seen, he goes on to explain that we are tempted by our own evil desires. James' purpose is to ensure that Christians have no excuse before God if they succumb to temptation, and to prevent any suggestion that God is tainted by the evil involved in temptation. It would be impossible for a Holy God to tempt a person to evil whilst maintaining His own moral integrity.

The fact that God does not tempt His people to evil does not mean that it is against His will and purpose for them to be tempted. Everything that we experience in life is under the ultimate sovereign control of God. Whilst God does not directly tempt people to sin, as the sovereign God who is in control of all things He allows His people to be tempted and weaves these temptations into His overall purposes. This is a sub-set of the wider problem of evil, which questions how a sovereign God can permit evil in the world without thereby becoming morally responsible for it. God is not the author of sin and evil, but He sovereignly uses demonic and human evil to accomplish His good purposes, as was the case with the suffering of Joseph[74] and supremely the crucifixion of Jesus.[75]

God's sovereignty over temptation, without ever being responsible for it, is evident in numerous instances in the Old and New Testament. Adam and Eve were not tempted by God

---

73. James 1:13.
74. Genesis 50:20.
75. Acts 2:22-24.

in the Garden of Eden, but God had created the serpent[76] and was fully aware that he would seek to tempt them and lead them into rebellion against Him. As the account of the Tower of Babel makes clear, God knows everything that is happening on earth, and He could have stepped down at any moment to prevent the serpent misleading Eve, or Eve eating the fruit of the tree of the knowledge of good and evil.[77] He chose not to, presumably to reveal the full extent of His grace and love in the salvation that would be necessary to reverse the fall of humanity, thus bringing Himself greater glory.

In the same way, we read how God allowed Satan to tempt and test Job by inflicting him with suffering, so as to prove that his faith was not simply the result of the blessings that he had received from God.[78] God similarly allowed Satan to tempt David to take a census of the fighting men of Israel towards the end of his reign, a sinful act of pride, autonomy and self-assertion that was even more serious than his adultery with Bathsheba.[79] Whilst God did not tempt Jesus, it was the Holy Spirit who led Jesus into the wilderness to be tempted by Satan,[80] so that He could win the victory over him and succeed where Adam and Israel had both failed.

God's sovereignty means that we can be sure that 'in all things God works for the good of those who love him,'[81] and that our sufferings and temptations are part of His eternal plan to conform us to the likeness of His Son the Lord Jesus. James is therefore able to encourage the Christians he is addressing

---

76. Genesis 3:1.
77. Genesis 11:5.
78. Job 1:12 and 2:6.
79. 1 Chronicles 21:1.
80. Mark 1:12.
81. Romans 8:28-30.

to rejoice in the sufferings and persecution they are facing because they know that this will produce resilient faith:

> Consider it pure joy, my brothers and sisters, whenever you face trials of many kinds, because you know that the testing of your faith produces perseverance. Let perseverance finish its work so that you may be mature and complete, not lacking anything.[82]

The term that James used for 'trials' is the same as that he uses for 'temptations' later in the chapter. In God's sovereignty, the challenges that we face in life, whether from external circumstances or internal temptations, serve the good purpose of deepening our faith, proving that it is genuine, and thereby bring glory to God. As Peter writes in his first letter, the trials that Christians experience:

> ... have come so that the proven genuineness of your faith – of greater worth than gold, which perishes even though refined by fire – may result in praise, glory and honour when Jesus Christ is revealed.[83]

The fact that we experience temptation does not mean that God has failed us, or that in some way Satan has been able to outmanoeuvre Him. Nor does it mean that God is playing games with us and that He is not a good and holy God. Instead every temptation is an opportunity provided by God to test our faith, and to prove its genuineness both to ourselves and a watching world. Victory over temptation brings both assurance of faith and greater maturity to the believer, but also greater glory to God.

---

82. James 1:2-4.
83. 1 Peter 1:7.

The sovereignty of God over temptation also means that we can have confident hope when we are experiencing temptation, because He promises to make it possible for us to stand firm and avoid falling into sin. As Paul writes in 1 Corinthians 10 verse 13:

> No temptation has overtaken you except what is common to mankind. And God is faithful; he will not let you be tempted beyond what you can bear. But when you are tempted, he will also provide a way out so that you can endure it.

Whilst we might find the doctrine of the sovereignty of God over temptation difficult, the alternative is infinitely less palatable, as it would mean that we could have no confidence that God is able to protect us from temptation and bring us safely into His eternal kingdom, nor would we have any grounds for thinking that the temptations and sufferings we experience have any meaning or beneficial purpose.

WHY DOES GOD ALLOW US TO BE TEMPTED?

Whatever good is to be attained, struggle is necessary. So do not fear temptations, but rejoice in them, for they lead to achievement. God helps and protects you. (St Barsanuphius)

My temptations have been my masters in divinity ... Temptation and adversity are the two best books in my library. (Martin Luther)

Whilst God does not tempt us Himself, the Bible makes clear that He allows us to be tempted. All temptation occurs under His sovereign superintendence and providential ordering of our world, and it is never contrary to His will or control. This raises the inevitable question as to why God allows us to be tempted. Although we cannot know the precise purpose of

God in every specific instance of temptation, because this has not been revealed to us in His Word, the Bible would suggest that there are at least two reasons why God allows us to be tempted, which are closely interconnected. Every temptation is a test of our faith, and so God allows us to be tempted to reveal His glory to others and to refine our faith.

The book of Job records the tempting of God's servant by both Satan and the 'friends' who seek to explain the reason for the sufferings he has experienced.[84] The opening chapters of the book reveal the heavenly background to the earthly sufferings that Job experiences. God allows Satan to test Job with suffering to prove, to both Satan and the watching audience of heavenly beings, that Job trusts God not just because of the material blessings he has received. God allows Satan to take away Job's material possessions and children, followed by his own health, in order to prove that Job will not curse Him.[85] Job's suffering is entirely innocent, but he is further provoked by his wife, who urges him to curse God,[86] and by his friends, who demand that he repent because they are convinced that he must have sinned and is therefore suffering the just judgement of God.[87] In the event, Job does sin, by charging God with injustice for not vindicating him,[88] but he does not curse God. Even in his greatest anguish and frustration with God he continues to trust Him and look for redemption and vindication, whether in this life or by way of resurrection from the dead.[89] The result is that God is

---

84. For the best accessible commentary on Job see Christopher Ash, Job: The Wisdom of the Cross, (Crossway Books, 2014).
85. Job 1-2.
86. Job 2:9.
87. Job 4-25.
88. Job 32-37; 40:4-5; 42:1-6.
89. Job 19:25.

vindicated, and Satan's charge that people only trust in Him because of what they can get from Him is exposed to be false. Job is ultimately restored by God, and receives more than he had ever lost, which is a picture of the resurrection and eternal blessings in the new creation that all Christians will receive along with Christ.[90]

The story of Job teaches us that our temptations, which may be so severe that they cause us to consider abandoning faith in God, are a way in which He brings glory to Himself by demonstrating that we do not trust in Him simply because of what we get from Him, but because of who He is. This will only become fully clear in eternity, when God has vindicated us, and Satan and those who have tempted us will be shown to have failed.

As well as bringing glory to God by demonstrating the true nature of our faith to others, the Bible also suggests that our temptations are a means by which God seeks to bring us to greater maturity and personal assurance of faith. This is made clear in 1 Peter, which was written to suffering Christians who were tempted to abandon their faith in Christ and return to their prior pagan life. Peter writes to encourage them to stand firm in the true grace of God that they have received. He reminds them that suffering for the sake of Christ is not an indication that God has let them down, nor that they have failed in their faith. Rather they are following in the footsteps of the Lord Jesus, who suffered innocently and unjustly. Peter characterizes the sufferings they are enduring as a 'test' that will refine their faith and prove, both to them and to others, that it is genuine:

90. Job 42:1-17.

> In all this you greatly rejoice, though now for a little while you may have had to suffer grief in all kinds of trials. These have come so that the proven genuineness of your faith – of greater worth than gold, which perishes even though refined by fire – may result in praise, glory and honour when Jesus Christ is revealed.[91]

It is often the hardships of life, and the inevitable temptations that accompany them, that are the greatest periods of spiritual growth. As we fight temptation the 'dross' of our lives is burnt away, and we gain greater boldness and confidence in Christ, and we are forced to let go of those things which encumber our lives and inhibit our whole-hearted devotion to Christ.[92] Even our failures can be moments of significant growth to greater faithfulness. The fact that God allowed Peter to be tempted, deny Christ, repent and be restored was crucial to his spiritual formation to become the leader of the early church. Peter was forced to face the bankruptcy of his self-confidence, pride and sense of superiority to others, with the result that he was humbled and learned to rely on Christ for grace and strength.

When God allows us to be tempted, especially by suffering and tough circumstances, He has not abandoned us or withdrawn His fatherly love and care from us. Far from it! Hebrews assures us that the sufferings and hardships we face are God's discipline, in the sense of training rather than punishment, which will produce maturity and fruitfulness:

> Endure hardship as discipline; God is treating you as his children. For what children are not disciplined by their father? ... No discipline seems pleasant at the time, but painful. Later on, however, it produces a harvest of

---

91. 1 Peter 1:6-7.
92. Hebrews 12:1-3.

righteousness and peace for those who have been trained by it.[93]

God's purpose in allowing us to be tempted is not to disable us, but rather to heal us and bring us to full maturity and assurance of faith. It is for our good and for His ultimate glory.

> When through fiery trials thy pathways shall lie,
> My grace all sufficient will be thy supply;
> The flame shall not hurt thee, I only design
> Thy dross to consume and thy gold to refine.[94]

---

93. Hebrews 12:7, 11.
94. From the hymn 'How firm a foundation' by Bob Kauflin. Original words by 'K' in Rippon's Hymns (1787). Traditional American Melody. Public Domain.

3

THEOLOGICAL FOUNDATION: CAN WE RESIST TEMPTATION?

I can resist everything except temptation.
(Oscar Wilde)

I can do all things through him who gives me strength.
(The Apostle Paul, Phil. 4:13)

In the previous chapter we saw that temptation is an inevitable and normal experience for Christians. We live in a fallen world that has been handed over to the rule of Satan, with the result that his lies dominate the culture of the hostile territory we inhabit. At the same time, even as regenerated Christians who have received new life in Christ, we continue to exist in fallen human flesh, which is subject to all kinds of sinful desires. We face an enemy without and an enemy within. It is therefore no surprise that the New Testament describes the normal Christian life as a fight,[1] or a spiritual battle.[2]

---

1. 1 Corinthians 9:26; 2 Corinthians 10:4; 1 Timothy 1:18; 6:12; 2 Timothy 4:7.
2. Ephesians 6:10-20.

Given that the normal Christian life is an experience of constant temptation, the question that arises is not whether we can escape from temptation, but whether we are able to resist temptation. Is it inevitable that we will succumb to temptation and sin, or is it possible for us to resist temptation and so avoid sinning? In other words, is the call to resist temptation a command that can be obeyed or a command that is impossible to obey?

This is of course a pastorally very important issue. What is the point of Christians striving to resist temptation if this is ultimately futile? How are we to feel about our failures to resist temptation? Should they give us concern and cast doubt on the reality of our faith in Christ or does our failure simply confirm the reality of our fallen condition even after we have been born again? How ought we to exhort and encourage one another to persevere in this war against Satan and our fallen flesh if victory will always elude us? These questions require a theological and biblical answer.

IS IT POSSIBLE TO RESIST TEMPTATION?

In order to consider this issue, we need to start by tackling one of the most hotly disputed passages of the New Testament, namely Romans 7:14-25. In these verses Paul describes an extreme experience of struggle against sin and articulates the deep despair of a person who is unable to obey the law of God, even though they know it to be good and holy. Many Christians instantly identify with the experience that Paul describes in this passage and, encouraged by many traditional commentators, they take it that he is describing the 'normal Christian life'. On this reading Christians should expect a life of struggle and failure against the desires of our fallen flesh.

Paul writes:

We know that the law is spiritual, but I am unspiritual, sold as a slave to sin. I do not understand what I do. For what I want to do I do not do, but what I hate I do. And if I do what I do not want to do, I agree that the law is good. As it is, it is no longer I myself who do it, but it is sin living in me. For I know that good itself does not dwell in me, that is, in my sinful nature. For I have the desire to do what is good, but I cannot carry it out. For I do not do the good I want to do, but the evil I do not want to do – this I keep on doing. Now if I do what I do not want to do, it is no longer I who do it, but it is sin living in me that does it.

So I find this law at work: although I want to do good, evil is right there with me. For in my inner being I delight in God's law; but I see another law at work in me, waging war against the law of my mind and making me a prisoner of the law of sin at work within me. What a wretched man I am! Who will rescue me from this body that is subject to death? Thanks be to God, who delivers me through Jesus Christ our Lord!

Whilst it might feel comforting to read this passage as describing the normal Christian life, since such a reading will reassure us that our struggles and failures are only to be expected, a more careful reading of the verses in their context suggests that Paul is not seeking to provide a pastoral description of 'the normal Christian life'. The passage has too often been misread as a counter to perfectionist holiness teaching, which claims that Christians can achieve a status of 'entire sanctification' that will raise their spiritual life to a level at which they no longer experience any struggle against temptation because they have been fully delivered from any sinful desires.

However, Romans 7 was not written to counter such perfectionist or holiness teaching. Taken in its original context in the unfolding argument of the letter to the Romans, Paul teaches neither a doctrine of Christian perfection nor of perpetual failure. He presents a nuanced understanding of our present salvation and deliverance from sin, in which we are required to struggle against our sinful desires but empowered to resist them and put them to death by the Holy Spirit who is dwelling within us. This is both realistic and hopeful.

In some ways, it is exegetically easier to identify what Romans 7:14-25 is not about, rather than what it is about. The passage occurs in the middle of Paul's extended argument in Romans 5-8 about the way in which the death of Jesus has brought deliverance from sin. His gospel is not just a message of forgiveness and justification through the atoning death of Jesus, though it is certainly that,[3] but also a message of transformation and the need to live a new life through our union with the risen Lord Jesus, by the power of the Holy Spirit He has given to indwell us.

In context Romans 7:14-25 is a parenthetical digression answering the question of a potential objector to Paul's wider teaching, who assumes that he is implying that the law, which was given to God's people in the Old Testament, was in some way sinful rather than good and holy.

The main point that Paul is making is first set out in his thesis statement in Romans 7:1-6. There he explains that Christians, irrespective of whether they come from a Jewish or Gentile background, no longer live under the law. Rather they are to live to please God by the Holy Spirit. In just the same way that a wife is released from her obligations to her husband when she becomes a widow, Christians have been united with Christ in His death and resurrection, and so have

---

3. See Romans 3:21-4:25.

been released from any obligation to live under the law.[4] The thrust of his argument is summarized in verse 6:

> But now, by dying to what once bound us, we have been released from the law so that we serve in the new way of the Spirit, and not in the old way of the written code.

In Romans 7:7-25 Paul reassures his readers that this does not mean that he is saying the law was somehow deficient, before he picks up his major theme and describes the 'new way of the Spirit' in Romans 8. The structure of Romans 7 and 8 makes clear that it is the latter chapter that sets out 'the normal Christian life', whereas Romans 7:14-25 is a description of life under the law – a life that has now been rendered obsolete because of what God has done through the death and resurrection of Jesus.

Romans is primarily a discourse on salvation history, explaining how God has at long last fulfilled His covenant promises to His people in Jesus, and not a work of either systematic or pastoral theology. It also needs to be remembered that Paul does not intend to suggest that the new life Christians enjoy in the Spirit is in any way a lowering of the level of holiness that was demanded by the law. It is a higher level of holiness and love which fulfils the righteous requirement of the law.[5] The nature of this new life is set out in specific detail, for the context of the Christians living in first-century Rome, in Chapters 12-15.

Romans 7 is therefore best understood as a description of the battle against temptation experienced by those who do not live according to the Spirit, but in the old way of the law. It describes the hopeless struggle that takes place when

---

4. Romans 7:1-4.
5. Romans 13:8-10.

there is a clash between the desires of the fallen human flesh, and the demands of God's good and holy law. The presence of indwelling sin, which has corrupted fallen human flesh, makes it impossible to obey the law and to carry our good intentions into effect. The result is failure and frustration, with sin winning the battle because the innate desire to do evil overcomes the competing desire to do good.

Romans 7:14-25 is primarily a description of the life of Old Testament believers who, like the author of Psalm 119, rejoiced in the goodness of God's law and yet were unable to fulfil its obligations. The whole history of Israel under the old covenant reflects the dilemma described in Romans 7:14-25. God's people delighted in the law that was given to them at Mount Sinai, and expressed their desire to obey it, but repeatedly found that they were unable to do so. They were seduced into idolatry and the worship of foreign gods. They thus experienced the curses of the covenant, culminating in the 'death' of exile which separated them from the Promised Land and the presence of God in the temple.[6] They longed for a 'resurrection' that would bring them home and set them free.[7]

This interpretation fits with Paul's understanding of the purpose of the law in God's plan of salvation, which is most fully developed in Romans and Galatians. The law was never given by God as a means of overcoming sin and reversing the effects of the fall, but rather was given to reveal the depth of the problem of sin to God's people by transforming their unconscious sins into known transgressions.[8] In God's unexpected plan, which has only

---

6. See for example Deuteronomy 28-30 and Leviticus 26.
7. As for example in Ezekiel 37.
8. Romans 3:20; Galatians 3:19.

become fully clear now that Christ has come, the law was intended both to provoke and increase sin, but also to act like a slave who would bring the people of Israel to the Messiah when He finally came.[9]

The law thus revealed the inadequacy of the old covenant and pointed ahead to the new covenant under which, as we saw in the previous chapter, God would give His people new hearts and pour out His Holy Spirit on them. Now that the new covenant has come, and the Spirit has been given, it is no wonder that Christians are to live in the new way of the Spirit and not the old way of the law.

It is less clear exactly how Paul is intending to speak in these verses, but to some extent this is not crucial to the argument being made here. Paul seems to be speaking of his own personal experience, since he uses the first person 'I', and the passage culminates in a personal cry of anguish as he declares, 'What a wretched man I am!' If this is indeed his intention, he is speaking retrospectively of his pre-Christian experience as a zealous Pharisee,[10] who sought to live in obedience to the law in a way that has never been attempted by the majority of contemporary Christians.[11] However, many respected commentators regard Paul as using a rhetorical device in these verses, so that he is speaking not as himself but as personified Israel under the old covenant, or as Adam in the Garden of Eden, or even of both together.[12]

---

9. Galatians 3:23-4.

10. Although this does not fit with his description of his prior life in Judaism in Philippians 3:4-6.

11. As he does in his autobiography in Acts 26:4-11 and Philippians 3:4-6.

12. Recent commentators who have taken this approach include Douglas Moo, Tom Schreiner, N. T. Wright and John Stott. In fact, it is difficult to find a recent commentator who has taken the view that Paul is speaking purely autobiographically.

Given the salvation-historical structure of Romans, and the context of this passage, it is overly simplistic to regard Romans 7:14-25 as describing the life of a person prior to their conversion, and Romans 8 as describing what their life should be like as a Christian. Rather these passages describe two contrasting ways of living, namely the old way of battling indwelling sin and temptation by the law without the Spirit, which was the experience of the Israelites under the old covenant, and the new way of battling indwelling sin and temptation by the Spirit without the law, which ought to be the experience of Christians living under the new covenant. Unregenerate people cannot live in the way described in Romans 8 because they have not received the gift of the Spirit. However, regenerate Christians can fall back into trying to live in the 'old way' described in Romans 7:14-25 if they become legalists and cease to rely on the empowering work of the Holy Spirit in their battle against indwelling sin and temptation.

In summary, we should not regard Romans 7:14-25 as describing the normal Christian life, but rather take it as a description of struggling against indwelling sin and temptation by the law without the help of the Holy Spirit. It is no wonder that this is a hopeless struggle resulting in inevitable failure and despair, since the power of sin is greater than that of the unaided human will, even when it is informed by the law. Paul's whole point in Romans is that those who have trusted Christ are not condemned to live such a life of unremitting failure and frustration, because they have already been redeemed from the power of sin in their lives and are now able to live a new life in the Spirit.

The final cry of Romans 7:24, 'Who will rescue me from this body that is subject to death?' fails to reflect the inaugurated 'now' of salvation that Paul highlights in the rest of Romans, which once again confirms that this is not a passage describing the usual experience of Christians. When we look closely, rather than superficially, at the language of Romans 7:14-21, we see that neither Paul nor any of the other apostles speaks of the life of converted Christian believers in such stark and bleak terms. Life in Christ is not an unrelenting failure of doing the evil that we do not want to do, and not doing the good that we want to do. We were, after all, saved to do good works of love and service.[13] The pastoral purpose of Romans 7:14-25 is not to bring us assurance when we fail to resist temptation and fall into sin, by persuading us that this was inevitable, but rather to drive us to live the new life of the Spirit and not to ever think that we would want to try to resist temptation and indwelling sin in our own strength and by the law.

To take Romans 7:14-25 as the description of the 'normal Christian life' is ultimately to adopt an 'under-realized escapology'! It downplays the degree to which regenerate believers have been set free from the ruling power of sin in their lives. The cross and resurrection have begun to reverse God's judgement on humanity which gave sinners over to 'sin' as an enslaving master. The main thrust of Paul's letter to the Romans is to highlight the freedom we have in Christ to live a new life of obedience and love, fulfilling the law's demands.

We can resist temptation because we have been set free from sin

He breaks the power of cancelled sin,
He sets the prisoner free;
His blood can make the foulest clean;

---

13. See for example Ephesians 2:10; Titus 3:8.

His blood availed for me.
(Charles Wesley, 'O for a thousand tongues to sing')

In contrast to the picture of failure and despair described in Romans 7:14-25, which reminds Paul's readers of the unwinnable conflict between sin and the law, the rest of Romans describes the glorious salvation that is enjoyed by those who have put their trust in Christ, confessing Him as Lord and believing that God has raised Him from the dead.[14] Romans makes clear that Christians have not just had their sins forgiven, but they have been set free from the ruling power of sin in their lives.[15] They have become new creations,[16] and as such they are no longer in bondage to the desires that come from their fallen human flesh. This is the essential foundation for the Christian life, and the result is that Christians can resist temptation so that they do not carry the desires of their flesh into action. Using the language of James, with which we started this book, by the power of the Spirit they can resist their own evil desires, so that they do not conceive and give birth to sin.[17]

Paul wrote his letter to the Romans to several congregations that were meeting in the capital city of the Empire[18] ahead of a visit to garner their support for a planned missionary journey to Spain.[19] It seems that some, perhaps many, members of the churches in Rome were sceptical of Paul and his Gentile mission, and were suspicious of his 'law-free' gospel message. Paul therefore sets out the gospel that he proclaimed, which

---

14. Romans 10:9-10.

15. Romans 6:7, 14.

16. 2 Corinthians 5:17.

17. James 1:15.

18. Romans 16:1-24 suggests there were at least five house congregations in Rome.

19. Romans 15:23-9.

he insists is the gospel of God,[20] and anticipated some of their questions and objections to his message.[21] The gospel he preaches reveals the faithfulness of God to His covenant promises,[22] and the power of God for the salvation of everyone who believes it.

Central to the letter, therefore, is an exposition of the nature and scope of the salvation that the gospel brings. The heart of the gospel message is the declaration that Jesus is the long-expected Messiah, the Christ, and the divine Son of God.[23] He has accomplished salvation for His people, for all those who put their faith and trust in Him, irrespective of their racial or ethnic background,[24] by His faithfulness, sacrificial death on the cross and glorious resurrection.[25] We will briefly follow the outline of Romans 1-8, highlighting how Jesus has brought salvation from sin, and what this will mean for individual Christians.

Humanity under the rule of sin

As we saw in the previous chapter, sin is not simply wrong things that we do. Paul personifies sin as a slave master who rules over us. As he explains in Romans 1:18-3:20, as a result of the Fall God has handed every person over to the ruling power of sin, which produces in them 'the sinful desires of their hearts'.[26] Paul uses sexual lust, both heterosexual and homosexual, as a paradigm example of our slavery to sin, although he goes on to identify a wider range of other sins

---

20. Romans 1:1-4.
21. For example, in Romans 2:1; 3:1; 6:1; 9-11.
22. Romans 1:17; 9:6.
23. Romans 1:3-4.
24. Romans 1:14-17; 3:29-31.
25. Romans 3:21-26.
26. Romans 1:24.

which we commit because we have been handed over to this ruling power of sin.[27]

The fact that we have been handed over to the ruling power of sin strips us of our freedom to resist temptation, and the result is that we inevitably sin. The whole of humanity is therefore justly under the wrath of God. There is no one who is righteous before God, and everyone deserves to be eternally condemned on the last day.

This opening section of the letter establishes what it is that we need to be saved from. We need to be delivered from the condemnation and wrath of God that we deserve because we have sinned, and also from the ruling power of sin to which we have been subjected.

Christians are forgiven and justified by faith in Christ
In Romans 3:21-4:25 Paul explains how men and women, who are justly under condemnation, can be forgiven and justified by God. To be justified means to be acquitted and declared innocent by a judge, and this acquittal confers the status of being 'righteous'. The glorious good news of the gospel is that those who put their faith and trust in Jesus are justified by God and declared to be righteous. Their sins are forgiven and they are no longer under condemnation.[28] This verdict is only possible because Jesus Christ was fully obedient to God and was entirely without sin. He was therefore able to offer Himself as an atoning sacrifice, bearing in Himself the death penalty that sin justly deserves.[29] Just as the Passover lamb took away the judgement that the Israelites deserved when the LORD struck down the firstborn

---

27. Romans 1:29-32.
28. Romans 8:1.
29. Romans 3:24; 8:3.

in Egypt,[30] so Jesus takes away judgement on behalf of all those who put their faith in Him as the risen Lord. They are cleansed by His blood and counted perfectly righteous in the eyes of God because His perfect obedience and faithfulness are counted to them. Jesus was a willing substitute who gave His life for them. Those who put their faith and trust in Jesus therefore enjoy a restored relationship with God. They are no longer alienated from Him, but have been reconciled to Him and they are at peace with Him.[31]

The forgiveness and justification that is enjoyed by all who trust in Christ is received by faith alone, and not by works or by religious rituals such as circumcision.[32] Justification by faith and the forgiveness of sins was nothing new, but had always been God's way of dealing with His people. Abraham and David were both justified by their faith in God's promises, and experienced the blessing of forgiveness.[33] The example of Abraham proves that justification is by faith alone and not by works, since he was justified when he trusted God's promise that a son and heir would be born from his 'dead' body, a miracle paralleling and foreshadowing the resurrection of Jesus, before he was circumcised and hundreds of years before the law was given through Moses.[34]

Christians are freed from sin because they are united with Christ

One of the objections people had, and still have, to Paul's message of justification by faith alone was their assumption that

---

30. Exodus 11-12.
31. Romans 5:1-11.
32. Romans 4.
33. Romans 4:1-8.
34. Romans 4:10-11.

it provides no incentive for holy living and resisting temptation. If people are forgiven and justified by faith alone, without the need for any works, then why not just keep on sinning?[35] It seems to offer the spiritual equivalent of having your cake and eating it. Given that Paul says that the accumulation of sin before Jesus came and died only served to enhance and magnify God's glory, why not sin even more in order to increase the glory of God yet further?[36]

Paul answers these kinds of objections in Romans 5-6, where he makes clear that the salvation Christians receive in Christ involves much more than just justification by faith. It is never less than this, but it is always much more.

He had already hinted at this in chapter 3 verse 24, where he spoke not just of the atonement that was accomplished by the substitutionary death of Christ, but said that 'all are justified freely by his grace through the redemption that came by Christ Jesus'. Redemption is the language of freedom from slavery, which would have been a common and comprehensible metaphor for people in the first century but was also deeply rooted in the story of the Exodus, when God redeemed His people from slavery in Egypt and set them free from their bondage to Pharaoh so that they could serve and worship Him as their true master. For Paul, the gospel announces not just our forgiveness and justification, but also declares that we have been set free from slavery to sin so that we are able to serve God as we ought.

In Romans 5-6 Paul employs a different concept and develops the full implications of the faith that we put in Christ, which resulted in our justification. When a person puts their faith in Jesus as the risen Lord they do not simply receive

35. Romans 6:15.
36. Romans 6:1.

the benefit of justification; they also undergo a change. They are spiritually united with Him. This is symbolized by their baptism, which pictures their incorporation into Christ, and the effects of this union with Him. When a person is united with Christ by faith they are joined to Him in His death and resurrection, so that what happened to Jesus has spiritually happened to them. Paul thus writes:

> Or don't you know that all of us who were baptised into Christ Jesus were baptised into his death? We were therefore buried with him through baptism into death in order that, just as Christ was raised from the dead through the glory of the Father, we too may live a new life.[37]

A Christian is therefore someone who has been co-crucified with Christ, co-buried with Christ, and co-raised with Christ. Jesus died not only as our substitute, taking the penalty that we deserve, but also as our representative, so that what happened to Him is true of us when we put our faith in Him.

The wonderful result of our union with Jesus Christ in His death and resurrection is that we have been set free from the ruling power of sin in our lives. The bondage to sin that we were under, because God handed us over to sin, has been broken. As Paul puts it in Romans 6:6-7:

> For we know that our old self was crucified with him so that the body ruled by sin might be done away with, that we should no longer be slaves to sin – because anyone who has died has been set free from sin.[38]

The consequence of this glorious and mysterious union of Christians with Christ is that we are now able to 'live a new

---

37. Romans 6:3-4.
38. Romans 6:6-7. See also Galatians 2:20 and 6:14.

life'[39] which is not dominated by sin. We cannot go on sinning because we have 'died to sin' and cannot live in it any longer.[40] The new freedom that we have been given entitles us to resist temptation and the sinful desires that still come from our fallen human bodies:

> Therefore do not let sin reign in your mortal body so that you obey its evil desires. Do not offer any part of yourself to sin as an instrument of wickedness, but rather offer yourselves to God as those who have been brought from death to life; and offer every part of yourself to him as an instrument of righteousness. For sin shall no longer be your master, because you are not under the law but under grace.[41]

What Paul is describing here is the new birth and new creation that takes place when a person is regenerated and comes to faith in Christ. It is not just that they are forgiven, but that they are given spiritual rebirth from the dead and are transferred from the kingdom of Satan to the kingdom of Jesus, and from the era of sin, death and the law to the era of grace and the Spirit. This wonderful renewal is not the grounds of our forgiveness and justification, because God loves us and justifies us when we are ungodly and in rebellion to Him.[42] Our salvation is a sheer act of undeserved sovereign grace. However, our new birth and spiritual resurrection with Christ sets us free from sin and enables us to be transformed by the renewing of our minds so that we can choose to offer our bodies as a living sacrifice that is holy and pleasing to God.[43]

---

39. Romans 6:4.
40. Romans 6:2.
41. Romans 6:12-14.
42. Romans 4:5; 5:8.
43. Romans 12:1-2.

In the light of what Paul says about the union of Christians with Christ in Romans 6, and the freedom that this brings, it is inconceivable that in Romans 7:14-25 he is describing the 'normal' Christian life as he understands it. The 'wretched man' of these verses, whoever he may be, is hardly a picture of someone who is living a new life, and who has been set free from their slavery to sin. Far from refusing to allow sin to reign in his mortal body he is someone who cannot do anything but obey the evil desires of his flesh. He seems to be incapable of offering himself to God and using his body as an instrument of righteousness rather than evil. He has not experienced the liberation that comes from being co-crucified, co-buried, and co-raised with Christ, but is still longing for deliverance from the fallen body of death.

This is just further confirmation that the argument above is correct, namely that Romans 7 describes the unwinnable conflict between the flesh and the law, rather than the normal Christian life which consists of a fierce struggle between the desires of the fallen flesh and the Holy Spirit. It is this to which Paul turns in Romans 7-8.

Christians can resist indwelling sin by the power of the Spirit

Whilst Paul makes clear that the salvation Christians experience by faith in Christ extends beyond justification and forgiveness to encompass redemption from slavery to sin, he is careful to avoid an over-realized eschatology that suggests that they are freed from the need to struggle against sin. As has already been explained, even though Christians have been regenerated, recreated and resurrected to new spiritual life, they continue to be embodied in fallen flesh, which is the source of sinful desires and temptations. They still find themselves in a battle against sin, which continues to dwell in their flesh. They have received the promised blessings of the new covenant, namely a new heart and the gift of the Spirit, so they are no longer fallen in the way in which they were before they exercised faith in Christ. The image of God is being renewed in them as they are remade into the likeness of their creator.[44] At their conversion they took off the old self and put on the new self in Christ.

However, they will not be freed from the struggle against sin until their flesh is transformed into the likeness of the glorious resurrection body of the Lord Jesus, which will happen at the end of this present age.[45] For the meantime, Christians inhabit two eras simultaneously, as the old age of sin and death overlaps with the new age of resurrection and the Spirit. Only if we grasp this will we be able to understand the true nature of the Christian life and learn how we are meant to resist the temptations that assail us. This is exactly what Paul sets out in Romans 7-8, and more concisely in Galatians 5:13-26 where he describes the new life in the Spirit that Christians are intended to enjoy.

Romans 8:1-17 picks up where Paul left off in Romans 7:6, and sets out what it means to serve 'in the new way of the Spirit and not in the old way of the written code.' The normal Christian life presented in Romans 8 is meant to be a stark contrast with the sub-Christian life described in Romans 7:14-25.

Paul begins by reminding his readers that Christians do not earn their forgiveness and justification because they live a new life in the Spirit. Christians are no longer under

---

44. Romans 8:29; Ephesians 4:24; Colossians 3:10.
45. 1 Corinthians 15:50-57.

condemnation because of what Christ has done for them.[46] God sent His Son 'to be a sin offering', so that sin would be condemned and punished in His flesh.[47] This reiterates what Paul said about forgiveness and justification by faith in Christ on the basis of His substitutionary death in chapter 3. The sacrificial death of Christ alone reverses the verdict of condemnation that we deserve, but also sets us free from 'the law of sin and death',[48] with the result that 'the righteous requirements of the law might be fully met in us'.[49]

Paul then goes on to explain that we can only enjoy this freedom from sin and fulfil the righteous requirement of the law if we live 'according to the Spirit' rather than according to the flesh. In Romans 8:5-8 he makes clear that regenerate Christians, who are no longer under condemnation and who have been set free from sin through the death of Christ, continue to experience a struggle against sin in their lives. They still have a fallen human flesh, which generates sinful desires. However, they also have the Holy Spirit dwelling within them, and the Holy Spirit produces competing desires to please God and obey His righteous requirements. This struggle between the desires of the flesh and the Spirit is clearly not the same struggle that is described in Romans 7:14-25, which makes no reference to the desires of the Holy Spirit. Romans 8 makes no reference to the Mosaic Law, which was a central theme of Romans 7.

The key question for the Christian is therefore which of these conflicting desires will gain mastery and determine their behaviour? Will it be sin or the Spirit that wins out?

---

46. Romans 8:1.
47. Romans 8:3, echoing 3:24.
48. Romans 8:2.
49. Romans 8:4.

The vital battleground is in the mind, and Christians have to choose to set their mind on the desires of the Spirit rather than the desires of the flesh:

> Those who live according to the flesh have their minds set on what the flesh desires; but those who live in accordance with the Spirit have their minds set on what the Spirit desires. The mind governed by the flesh is death, but the mind governed by the Spirit is life and peace. The mind governed by the flesh is hostile to God; it does not submit to God's law, nor can it do so. Those who are in the realm of the flesh cannot please God.[50]

Paul's teaching here makes it absolutely clear that the normal Christian life is a battle against the sinful desires of the flesh, which tempt us to sin. Some Christians, notably John Wesley and subsequent holiness teachers who have come after him, have suggested that it is possible for Christians to attain a state of entire sanctification or perfection, when they will be completely free from the desires of sin and no longer have to endure this battle.[51] However, Paul gives no support for this idea, nor do any of the other New Testament authors.

Paul's description of the normal Christian life as a battle between the competing desires of indwelling sin in our flesh and the indwelling Holy Spirit, is confirmed in Galatians 5:13-26 where, after an extensive argument demonstrating that the age of the law has been displaced by the new age of the Spirit,[52] he urges the Galatians to 'walk by the Spirit', and produce the fruit of the Spirit rather than committing the acts of the flesh. In 5:16-17 he explains the

---

50. Romans 8:5-8.
51. For an overview of John Wesley's teaching see Melvin E Deiter, 'The Wesleyan Perspective' in *Five Views on Sanctification*, Zondervan 1987.
52. Galatians 3:1–4:31.

struggle between the flesh and the Spirit that we have also seen in Romans 8:

> So I say, live by the Spirit, and you will not gratify the desires of the flesh. For the flesh desires what is contrary to the Spirit, and the Spirit what is contrary to the flesh. They are in conflict with each other, so that you are not to do whatever you want.

Whilst the normal Christian life is a struggle between the sinful desires of our fallen human flesh, and the righteous desires of the Holy Spirit, who is Himself God and therefore reflects God's perfect holy character, Paul's point in both Romans and Galatians is that the Spirit empowers Christians to resist the desires of the flesh. The Christian is not someone who lives in the realm of the flesh, but in the realm of the Spirit, so it is not inevitable that their mind will be governed and ruled by the desires of the flesh. The Spirit has brought life rather than death, and Christians who allow the Spirit to govern their mind are able to submit to the righteous requirements of the law and live to please God. Paul therefore urges Christians to live by yielding to the controlling influence of the Spirit, which is pictured as 'living in accordance with the Spirit', 'walking by the Spirit', being 'led by the Spirit' and keeping 'in step with the Spirit'.

The Holy Spirit enables Christians to radically renounce, reject and repress the desires of the flesh, so that they do not act on them. Paul uses the very vivid language of execution to describe the way in which we are to suppress the desires of the flesh by the Spirit. In Romans 8:12-13 he writes:

> Therefore, brothers and sisters we have an obligation – but it is not to the flesh, to live according to it. For if you live

according to the flesh, you will die; but if by the Spirit you put to death the misdeeds of the body, you will live.

Paul uses very similar language in Galatians, where he speaks of how 'those who belong to Christ Jesus have crucified the flesh with its passions and desires.'[53] In his letters to the Ephesians and Colossians he uses a different metaphor to make the same point, comparing our fallen human nature to a set of clothes that we have taken off, so that we can be re-clothed in the new self that is being recreated by the Spirit in the likeness of Christ.[54]

The primary pastoral application of Paul's teaching in both Romans and Galatians is that Christians, who are by definition indwelt by the Holy Spirit,[55] cannot possibly continue living a life of sin, indulging and gratifying the desires of their fallen human flesh. He expects them to enjoy victory over the temptations that come from their flesh and to live in obedience to God.

They do not do this to earn their salvation, or even to prove their salvation. It is the inevitable outworking of the fact that they have been redeemed by Christ. This is the answer to the objection raised to Paul's 'law-free' gospel message, namely that it provides no incentive for restraining sin and promoting holiness of life and good works. Far from being the case, those who have received salvation through the gospel, who have been forgiven and justified, have also been set free from the ruling power of sin so that they can live a new life of service and obedience. Anyone who continues to live according to the flesh, indulging their sinful desires and misusing their bodies in the service of wickedness, is

---

53. Galatians 5:24.
54. Ephesians 4:22-24; Colossians 3:5-14.
55. Romans 8:9.

thereby showing that they are not indwelt by the Spirit, and that they are not in fact Christians at all. Regeneration, union with Christ and the gift of the Spirit inevitably result in a new life that fulfils the law.

Christians will ultimately share in the glory of the new creation

The normal Christian life, of struggle against the sinful desires of our flesh in the power of the Spirit, reflects the current era of salvation history. The old age of sin, death and the law is overlapping with the new age of grace, resurrection life and the Spirit. Whilst Christians can expect to enjoy victory over temptation and sin, they will not be free from the battle, which continues day by day, hour by hour and minute by minute. Many Christians enjoy a far greater measure of victory in this battle than they imagine, as is evidenced by the huge range of temptations that they resist. However, they easily become wearied and discouraged by the prolonged conflict and the absence of any rest from the heat of battle.

Christians should never lose sight of the hope that this battle will one day finally be over. Paul ends the section of his letter to the Romans that runs from chapter 5 to chapter 8 with a reminder of the sure and certain hope that Christians have that their present struggles and suffering will come to an end. The overlap of the ages will not continue for eternity. Jesus will return and His people will share in His glory. The entire creation will be redeemed and liberated from its current bondage to decay, which is the result of human sin and the just judgement of God. Our own fallen human bodies will be redeemed, and resurrected or transformed into the likeness of Jesus' glorious resurrection body.[56] When that happens we will be totally free from the temptations that come from the sinful desires of our fallen flesh. There will no longer be any struggle against sin, and we will no longer need to put to death the misdeeds of the body or to crucify the desires of the flesh. Not only will we be set free from our internal temptations, but the Book of Revelation assures us that Satan himself will be judged and cast into the lake of fire, so that there will no longer be any tempter to seek to persuade us to rebel against God.[57]

We can be absolutely sure that we will experience this final and complete redemption, because God is sovereign, almighty and faithful to His promises. As Paul writes in Romans 8:28-30:

> And we know in all things God works for the good of those who love him, who have been called according to his purpose. For those God foreknew he also predestined to be conformed to the image of his Son, that he might be the firstborn amongst many brothers and sisters. And those he predestined, he also called; those he called, he also justified; those he justified, he also glorified.

If we have received God's call, and trusted in Christ, our future redemption and glorification is so certain that Paul is able to speak about it in a prophetic past tense. There is no power, being or circumstance in the whole of the cosmos – whether earthly or heavenly, spiritual or material – that can subvert God's purpose and separate us from His love in Christ.[58] In the meantime, as we live in hope and continue to struggle against

---

56. 1 Corinthians 15.
57. Revelation 20:7-10.
58. Romans 8:38-9.

sin and endure suffering, God is present with us by His Spirit to help us in our weaknesses, reassuring us that we are the sons of God with a wonderful inheritance ahead[59] and interceding for us when we do not know what we ought to pray for.[60] The result is that we are able to triumph in the battle, enduring to the end and emerging as 'more than conquerors'.

Living the normal Christian life

This examination of Paul's teaching from Romans, aided by his parallel material in Galatians, has given us a picture of the normal Christian life. To summarize, Christians continue to battle against temptation and sinful desires because they still have a fallen human flesh. However, they have been redeemed by Christ from the ruling power of sin, so that they are no longer obliged to indulge or gratify those desires. Instead they are indwelt by the Holy Spirit, who generates competing new desires to please God and fulfil the righteous requirements of His good and holy law. They have to choose whether their minds, and therefore their actions, will be governed by the sinful desires of their flesh or the righteous desire of the indwelling Spirit. The Spirit will empower them to put the desires of the flesh to death so that they do not act upon them. This struggle will continue until the end of the age, when Jesus returns, and we are resurrected to glory and finally experience the fullness of redemption and salvation.

This picture of the Christian life is reiterated in other New Testament letters and underlies every exhortation and command to do good or live a holy life. They teach that Christians have not just been forgiven but have been

---

59. Romans 8:14-17.
60. Romans 8:26-7.

regenerated to a new life in Christ.[61] In Titus, for example, Paul writes that the grace of God:

> teaches us to say 'No' to ungodliness and worldly passions, and to live self-controlled, upright and godly lives in this present age.[62]

The author of Hebrews assumes that the Christians he is addressing will be able, with the help of Christ their great high priest, to resist the temptation to abandon their faith and return to Judaism despite the growing threats of persecution they are facing. James presupposes that his readers will be able to avoid allowing their temptations to give birth to sin.[63]

Peter assumes that his regenerate readers still experience 'sinful desires' that war against their souls, but urges them to abstain from them. He commands them to stop 'living in debauchery, lust, drunkenness, orgies, carousing and detestable idolatry'[64] as they had when they were still pagan. To translate this into the Pauline idiom, he is asking them to mortify the desires of their flesh and to use their bodies in the service of righteousness. In his second letter he assures his Christian readers that, in the Lord Jesus and the gospel, they already have 'everything we need for a godly life'[65] and so urges them to:

> ... make every effort to add to your faith goodness, and to goodness, knowledge; and to knowledge, self-control; and to self-control, perseverance; and to perseverance

---

61. John 1:13; 3:3; James 1:18; 1 Peter 1:3.
62. Titus 2:12.
63. James 1:15.
64. 1 Peter 2:11; 4:2-3.
65. 2 Peter 1:3.

godliness; and to godliness, mutual affection; and to mutual affection, love.[66]

Peter's commands and exhortations would be both incoherent and impossible if Romans 7:14-25 were a description of the normal Christian life.

This compelling picture ought to bring great hope and encouragement to Christians. The fact that we experience temptations and sinful desires is not a sign that we are failing in our Christian life, nor that we lack spiritual maturity. The crucial question is whether we are resisting the desires we experience, putting them to death and choosing to live according to the desires of the Holy Spirit so that we love and serve God.

The glorious truth that we live in the new covenant era of the Spirit, and not under the law, means that our struggle against sin is not futile and merely symbolic. We are not in the hopeless condition of the wretched man described in Romans 7, who cannot fulfil the righteous requirement of the law because he has no power to overcome the desires of the flesh. Each time we choose to resist our sinful desires, which tempt us to sin, we are experiencing victory over sin by the power of the Holy Spirit.

> O how the grace of God
> amazes me!
> It loosed me from my bonds
> and set me free!
> What made it happen so?
> His own will, this much I know,
> set me, as now I show,
> at liberty.

---

66. 2 Peter 1:5-7.

Come now, the whole of me,
eyes, ears and voice,
join me, creation all,
with joyful noise:
praise him who broke the chain
holding me in sin's domain
and set me free again!
Sing and rejoice!
(E. T. Sibomana, 'O How the Grace of God Amazes Me')

4

PRACTICAL APPLICATION: HOW DO WE RESIST TEMPTATION?

The man who decides to struggle against his flesh and to overcome it by his own efforts is fighting in vain. The truth is that unless the Lord overturns the house of the flesh and builds the house of the soul, the man wishing to overcome it has watched and fasted for nothing. (John Climacus)

In the last two chapters we have laid the theological foundations that are essential to understanding why we experience temptation as Christians, and how we are able to resist temptation. Whilst we continue to live in our fallen human flesh, we have been redeemed from the ruling power of sin through the death and resurrection of the Lord Jesus, and we are indwelt by the Holy Spirit, who give us new desires to love and serve God and empowers us to resist the desires of our flesh. We are not condemned to a life of perpetual failure and sin, but rather have the confident hope that we can be 'more than conquerors'[1] and enjoy a life of victory over temptation and sin.

The question remains as to how we apply these biblical principles in our day-to-day struggles against temptation. In this much more applicational chapter we will consider what it means in practice to mortify the desires of the flesh and resist temptation, so that our temptations do not give birth to full-blown sin. We will try to synthesize a wide range of New Testament teaching and draw on examples from the history of Israel which, Paul tells us, occurred as examples for us and were written down as warnings to us.[2]

We will see that we need to take both protective and prophylactic steps to diminish the opportunity for temptation, alongside radical steps of resistance and renunciation of the temptations that afflict us. Negatively we have to 'put to death the misdeeds of the body,'[3] and positively we need to clothe ourselves with the Lord Jesus Christ so that we 'do not think about how to gratify the desires of the flesh.'[4]

There is no single simple way to fight against temptation, and no silver bullet to give us the victory. Rather the Bible teaches we must fight the battle against sin on multiple fronts at the same time. It is the mutual interaction of these different strategies that together enables us to mortify the flesh and resist temptation.

BE ON YOUR GUARD

Be thoroughly acquainted with your temptations and the things that may corrupt you – and watch against them all

---

1. Romans 8:37.
2. 1 Corinthians 10:1-11.
3. Romans 8:13.
4. Romans 13:14.

day long. You should watch especially the most dangerous of the things that corrupt, and those temptations that either your company or business will unavoidably lay before you. (Richard Baxter)

As we have seen in the earlier chapters, facing temptation is an inevitable experience for Christians because we live in a fallen world and dwell in our fallen human flesh. There is a sense in which temptation should never, therefore, take us by surprise. We need to be on guard against temptation, expecting and anticipating it, and taking preventative measures in advance. To be forewarned is to be forearmed.

We are most likely to succumb to our temptations if we complacently assume that we will be able to resist them. Paul warned the Corinthian Christians:

So, if you think you are standing firm, be careful that you don't fall![5]

Peter yielded to temptation and denied Christ three times when put under pressure precisely because of his arrogant overconfidence that he was stronger than others and would be willing to die with Jesus.[6]

If we are to resist temptation we need to be suspicious of ourselves and distrustful of our ability to stand firm. We need to know that we are weak in ourselves, and that we will need the help and power of the Holy Spirit to resist temptations. We need to be honest about our vulnerability and order our lives accordingly. We need to recognize that sin is inherently attractive to our flesh and offers us short-term pleasure and self-fulfilment.

---

5. 1 Corinthians 10:12.
6. Matthew 26:31-35; 69-75.

TAKE PERSONAL RESPONSIBILITY

> *I am tempted to think that I am now an established Christian,*
> *– that I have overcome this or that lust so long, that I have*
> *got into the habit of the opposite grace, – so that there is no*
> *fear; I may venture very near the temptation – nearer than*
> *other men. This is a lie of Satan. One might as well speak of*
> *gunpowder getting by habit of resisting fire, so as not to catch*
> *spark.* (Robert Murray McCheyne)

The temptations we experience flow from our fallen human flesh, satanic influence in our culture or direct satanic suggestion. The Bible makes clear that we alone are responsible for our sin, and that we have no excuse if we fail to resist temptation. If we fall into sin we cannot pass the buck and blame God, Satan or others for our failure.

In 1 Corinthians 10:13 Paul encourages Christians to remember that yielding to temptation is never inevitable:

> No temptation has overtaken you except what is common to mankind. And God is faithful; he will not let you be tempted beyond what you can bear. But when you are tempted, he will also provide a way out so that you can endure it.

In this passage Paul was drawing on the experience of the Israelites in the wilderness, where they had yielded to the temptations of idolatry, sexual immorality and doubt that God would enable them to take possession of the Promised Land. He makes clear that there was nothing inevitable about the failure of the Israelites. God had provided a way in which they could have resisted these temptations. He applies this example to the Corinthians, who were being tempted to keep attending idol feasts at the pagan temples with their friends or engaging in the sexual immorality for which the city was notorious. He wanted them to know that they had an alternative to sinning in these ways. He warns them that resisting temptation may be costly, but it is never impossible. The reason we give in to temptation is that we think the cost of resistance is greater than the cost of indulgence.

This means that the Christian who is tempted, for example, to view internet pornography, commit adultery, engage in homosexual sex, cut their church-giving in favour of a luxurious holiday, or keep silent when there is an opportunity to speak of Christ to a work colleague, cannot blame anyone but themselves if they give in and sin. The promise of God's Word means that we can be sure that whenever we are tempted, no matter how powerful that temptation might be, God has provided a way for us to resist and to 'say no to ungodliness'.[7]

However, whilst God always provides a 'way out' from sinning, this does not mean that He provides an easy way out. The way out that enables us to resist temptation may involve considerable personal cost and suffering, even to the point of death. This should not surprise us, since the way out that God provided for Jesus from temptation in the Garden of Gethsemane was for Him to go the way of the cross, and to give His life as a ransom for many. In the Old Testament, for example, Joseph was only able to resist the temptation to commit adultery with his master's wife by fleeing from her, which enabled her to make false accusations against him and landed him in prison.[8] Shadrach, Meshach and Abednego were only able to resist the temptation to bow down to the golden image erected by Nebuchadnezzar by being willing to

---

7. Titus 2:12.
8. Genesis 39.

be thrown into the fiery furnace.[9] The only way out open to Daniel from the temptation not to pray to the LORD because of King Darius' order was to be thrown in the lions' den.[10] All of these men were willing to cast themselves on the mercy of God rather than yield to temptation, not knowing with certainty whether God would save them or not. Whilst many Old Testament saints who resisted temptation were delivered from death and suffering, the author of Hebrews reminds us that others were faithful to the point of death:

> Some faced jeers and flogging, and even chains and imprisonment. They were put to death by stoning; they were sawn in two; they were killed by the sword.[11]

We will only fight the battle against temptation if we are willing to suffer rather than to sin. This is the message of the New Testament, especially of 1 Peter. Peter was writing to Christians who were facing suffering and persecution in Rome. They had been marginalized and ostracized by their erstwhile pagan friends because of their new faith and the changes of lifestyle it had produced. They were facing increasing suspicion from the state, which was beginning to see them as a dangerous and subversive sect. Some of them, especially slaves with non-Christian masters, were experiencing physical suffering for their faith,[12] and it seems that some amongst them had been killed for their faith. Peter encouraged them that they were following in the footsteps of the Lord Jesus Himself, who had Himself suffered for doing good rather than doing evil, and who had been willing to

---

9. Daniel 3.
10. Daniel 6.
11. Hebrews 11:36-7.
12. 1 Peter 2:18-25.

suffer on the cross for our sins. He therefore urged them to follow His example:

> Therefore, since Christ suffered in his body, arm yourselves also with the same attitude, because whoever suffers in the body has finished with sin. As a result, they do not live the rest of their earthly lives for evil human desires, but rather for the will of God.[13]

The author of Hebrews made an almost identical point to his readers, who were Jewish Christians facing the temptation to avoid suffering for the sake of Christ by returning to Judaism:

> In your struggle against sin, you have not yet resisted to the point of shedding your blood.[14]

We will only be committed to resisting temptation if we have confidence that in each instance there is an option to refuse to sin, and that God has provided everything we need to be able to choose to take this way out. There is never 'no alternative' to sinning. There is always the option to refuse and run, even where the only alternative to sin is to die, as has been the choice of many martyrs who have refused to save their lives by renouncing Christ. We can never be overpowered by temptation because we have the greater power of the Holy Spirit dwelling within us. The power of temptation, no matter its source, is less than that of the power of God at work within us. As John writes, 'The one who is in you is greater than the one who is in the world.'[15] Sin only has the power over us that we willingly grant it. Sin's great deception is to claim more power over us than it really has.

---

13. 1 Peter 4:1-2.
14. Hebrews 12:4.
15. 1 John 4:4.

TAKE RADICAL ACTION

Learn to say no; it will be of more use to you than to be able to read Latin. (C. H. Spurgeon)

Whilst the Bible reassures us that we can always resist temptation, it is important that we recognize that resisting temptation is not something that happens automatically in our Christian lives. Unlike our regeneration and justification – which are solely the work of God as He gives us new birth, new life and faith, and declares us to be righteous – progress in holiness requires our active engagement and effort. We resist temptation by working and doing.

The New Testament language about fighting temptation and sin is replete with imperative commands that require us to act. As we have seen, we are called to live by the Spirit, but this requires us to consciously choose to be orientated and controlled by His leading and direction. Whilst our temptations arise spontaneously from our fallen flesh and engagement with the fallen world in which we are living, we will only resist them if we take strong and decisive action against them. As Jesus so graphically taught His disciples, in the context of resisting sexual lust:

> If your right eye causes you to stumble, gouge it out and throw it away. It is better for you to lose one part of your body than for your whole body to be thrown into hell. And if your right hand causes you to stumble, cut it off and throw it away. It is better for you to lose one part of your body than for your whole body to go into hell.[16]

As we have already seen, Paul told the Christians in Rome that they had to 'mortify' the desires of their flesh, meaning

---

16. Matthew 5:29-30.

to execute them or put them to death.[17] In effect to resist temptation we must wield the executioner's sword against our own desires. He similarly instructed the Christians in Crete to refuse to obey the sinful passions of their flesh.[18] Peter likewise urged Christians to escape the corruption in the world caused by evil desires.[19]

Whilst we contribute no effort of our own to our regeneration and justification, some Christians have mistakenly taught that we also resist temptation and attain sanctification by faith alone. They have claimed that full sanctification will be achieved if only we are fully consecrated to Christ and trust His promises of deliverance. This experience may take the form of a 'second blessing' that translates us to a higher level of spiritual life.

Whilst it is certainly the case, as we will see shortly, that resisting temptation requires that we trust the gospel promises of deliverance from sin, this is not sufficient in itself to defeat temptation. It is a prerequisite that makes it possible to resist sin, but it is not itself the way in which we ensure that temptation does not give birth to sin. We are required to act in faith and by the power of the Spirit. We must practise the spiritual equivalent of contraception or abortion on our sinful desires, preventing them from conceiving and giving birth to sin. Resisting temptation is not just a case of 'letting go and letting God'. We are soldiers on a battlefield who are fighting a vicious enemy, and we must take up the arms and armour that have been provided for us by our commanding general and use them to take the fight to the enemy.[20]

---

17. Romans 8:12-13.
18. Titus 2:11-14.
19. 2 Peter 1:3-4.
20. Ephesians 6:10-20.

Believe the promises of the gospel

As we saw in the last chapter, Christians have been redeemed from slavery by virtue of their union with Christ, which means that they share in the liberating victory of His death and resurrection. This is an objective reality, but it is one that we have to constantly appropriate and apply to our lives. We will fail to resist sin if we lose faith that we have been delivered from its mastery over us, and fall into thinking that we cannot do anything but succumb.

It is for this reason that Paul commanded the Roman Christians to:

> ... count yourselves dead to sin but alive to God in Christ Jesus.[21]

The language 'count yourself' is taken from the world of accountancy and means to do the sums and identify the bottom line. It involves identifying the truth and living in the light of it. Christians can live confident that they are righteous before God because the righteousness of Christ has been credited to their account,[22] and in just the same way we can be sure that we have been set free from our slavery to sin.

As we experience temptation and the pull towards disobedience and sin, we need to engage in the mental activity of remembering who we are in Christ, and that sin no longer has any right to rule over us. It is no longer our master and we owe it no obligation. We are free to refuse to allow it to reign over our bodies and to refuse to obey its evil desires.

As Christians, we are rather like footballers who have been transferred from one team to another. We wear a new shirt and have a new manager. Transferred players may feel

21. Romans 6:11.
22. Romans 4:3.

an emotional pull when playing against their old team and former teammates, or when they hear the voice of their previous coach. They need to remember the shirt they now wear, and the new allegiance they have. They have been sold, such that their old obligations have been terminated. Christians are in a similar position in relation to sin, and we need to remember and assert our new freedom. The answer to temptation is to say 'No'[23], but we will only be able to do this if we trust and believe that we have the right to do so.

I have an occasional recurring dream, in which I am at school about to take my A-level exams. As I enter the examination hall and turn over the paper I realize I am meant to have been studying Biology for the last two years and not History, so I am unable to answer any of the questions. The dream seems so vivid and real that when I wake up I have to remind myself of what is really true. I did pass my A-levels and went on to complete a degree and a post-graduate degree! This is what we need to do in the Christian life. We need to remind ourselves of what is true about us. We do not remind ourselves of our own achievements, but rather of what Christ has achieved for us, and what is credited to our account as a result of our union with Him in His death and resurrection by faith.

LOVE AND FEAR GOD

Our response to temptation is an accurate barometer of our love for God. (Erwin W. Lutzer)

All sin is ultimately rebellion against God, and a rejection of His good and sovereign rule over us, our circumstances and our world. The best protection against temptation is

---

23. Titus 2:12.

therefore to cultivate a right relationship with God, and the desire to serve, honour and obey Him. We are to fight the sinful desires of our fallen flesh by fostering new affections for God that make sin seem horrible and unattractive to us. It is not enough that we intellectually know that sin is wicked, nor that indulging temptation will bring pain and suffering to ourselves or to others. We need to overcome the desire to sin with a greater desire to love God and enjoy His goodness.

The fundamental duty we have as Christians is to love God with the whole of our being. Jesus taught that the greatest command is to:

> Love the Lord your God with all your heart and with all your soul and with all your mind.[24]

Prior to our regeneration we did not, and could not, love God as we ought. Deep down we hated and despised God and wished that He did not exist. We wanted to be god ourselves. We were His enemies and alienated from Him. However, as Christians we have been transformed so that we are able to love God. We love Him because He first loved us,[25] and He has poured His love into our hearts by His Holy Spirit.[26]

Love for God is not just love for the idea of God's attributes in the abstract, nor love for the blessings and benefits we receive from Him. It is love for God as He is in Himself. If we love God we will be captivated by, and delight in, His goodness and beauty. We will long to please Him, just as children long to please a parent they love. We will hate the idea of hurting and alienating Him, or of doing anything that might incur His displeasure and discipline.

---

24. Matthew 22:37.
25. 1 John 4:19.
26. Romans 5:5.

If we give in to temptation and choose to sin it is always fundamentally because we have not loved God more than we have loved ourselves. We have fallen for the deception that the short-term pleasure of sin[27] will be greater than the long-term pleasure of God. It is not a surprise that throughout the Bible the sin of God's people is characterized as spiritual adultery. God is the husband of His people, and they have strayed from Him because they have not loved Him enough but have found another to be more attractive to them.

Closely related to this need to love God is the equally important need to fear God. God is not our equal, still less our buddy. He is the omniscient, omnipotent and omnipresent sovereign Lord of the universe. He is the transcendent, glorious and holy creator, who hates sin and wickedness with a burning passion of purity. He is the perfectly just judge who will pour out His wrath against all evil. He is the jealous God who will not stand to share His glory with any other. According to the book of Proverbs, this right fear of God is the 'beginning of knowledge'[28] and the fountainhead of the wisdom that will equip us to avoid temptation and sin.

For Christians, fear of God is not terror of Him because He is capricious, over-demanding, harsh or strict, but rather an appropriate reverent awe for who He is. Nor is it fear of eternal punishment if we fall short of His perfect standards, as we surely do, because we know that there is now no condemnation for those who are in Christ Jesus. It is the natural response to His glory and His greatness, which occurs when we grasp just how far He has condescended to enter a relationship with us. It is a fear of the horrific consequences that would result if we were to yield to temptation and

27. Hebrews 11:25.
28. Proverbs 1:7.

abandon our faith in Christ. As the letter to Hebrews warns us, if we abandon faith in Christ so as to avoid suffering there is no other way to avoid the just judgement of God, and as a result 'it is a dreadful thing to fall into the hands of the living God.'[29] This proper fear underlies our duty to give Him praise and worship, to bow down before Him and honour His name. If we want to resist temptation, we need to know the power of expulsive fear, a fear of God that is greater than our fear of suffering or our fear of the opinions and actions of other people. As Jesus warned His disciples:

> Do not be afraid of those who kill the body but cannot kill the soul. Rather, be afraid of the One who can destroy both soul and body in hell.[30]

Fear of God in this positive sense is a vital protection against sin, and powerful motivation to resist our temptations, not merely because we fear His displeasure, but because we hate the thought of bringing Him dishonour. Love for God and fear for God will give us the desire to glorify God and honour His name. It will produce the passion to pray 'Our Father in heaven, hallowed by your name.'[31] It will make sin seem truly disgusting and horrific to us. As such it will serve as a great disincentive to sin and strong encouragement to mortification.

If we want to resist sin, we therefore need to cultivate deep love and fear of God. We do this by meditating on who He is and what He has done. He has revealed Himself to us through salvation history, but supremely and finally in His Son. We see the full extent of His love and awesome holiness most clearly

---

29. Hebrews 10:31.
30. Matthew 10:28.
31. Matthew 6:9.

at the cross, where His twin characteristics of compassionate mercy and justice are reconciled through the willing sacrifice of Jesus for our sins.[32] Our hearts ought to be moved to love God as we glimpse the full height, depth, breadth and width of His love for us,[33] and see the full force of His wrath and hatred of sin as He punishes Jesus in our place.

If you are struggling to resist temptation, and finding that you lack the resolve to fight, the root problem is that you do not yet love and fear God sufficiently. You need to fight sin by cultivating a new depth of love and fear for Him. Joseph was able to resist the sexual temptation of Potiphar's wife because of his knowledge of God and concern for His honour. When she invited him to come to bed with her, he replied:

> How then could I do such a wicked thing and sin against God?[34]

This is exactly what King David failed to do when he was attracted to Bathsheba.[35] His sin was ultimately a failure in his relationship with God.[36]

Hate sin and Satan

If we cultivate love and fear for God, and a deep concern for His honour and glory, the inevitable corollary will be that we begin to hate sin and the author of sin, namely Satan, with greater vehemence. One of the prime reasons that we give in to temptation rather than resisting our desires is because we have a trivial view of sin. We fall for the lie that it is not that serious and will not cause much harm. A light view of

---

32. Romans 3:26; 5:8.
33. Ephesians 3:17-19.
34. Genesis 39:9.
35. 2 Samuel 11:1-4.
36. 2 Samuel 12:7-10; Psalm 51:3-4.

sin will inevitably encourage us to enjoy the momentary pleasure that sin brings, by assuming that this comes at little real cost. This is especially true for sins that seem to have no immediate victims, as for example viewing pornography.

To counter this self-justification, whether conscious or unconscious, we need to cultivate an awareness of the true wickedness of sin. The Bible consistently uses strong language to describe the seriousness of sin – whether evil, wickedness, vileness, abomination and the like – and this needs to become our vocabulary for sin. One reason why we find this hard is because we find it difficult to maintain a compassionate love for sinners whilst at the same time regarding sin itself as horrific and morally repugnant. However, Jesus taught us that this is what we must do; just as He Himself hated sin and yet came to seek and save the lost.[37]

We can cultivate a right and proper hatred of sin by carefully considering the consequences of sin on individuals and the corporate life of society. Sexual infidelity, for example, leads to family breakdown, pain and poverty. The sex industry and pornography are inextricably linked to human trafficking and child abuse. Consumer self-indulgence and greed causes global inequality and environmental degradation. We ought to give thought to the full implications and consequences of our sinful actions.

However, the horror of sin is not first and foremost determined by utilitarian criteria, namely the degree of harm that it causes to other people. This is not the moral yardstick by which sin is to be viewed. The horror of sin derives ultimately from the fact that is an affront to the Holy and

---

37. Luke 19:10.

Almighty God.[38] It is an act of treason and rebellion against Him, and an insult to both His right to rule and His goodness. Sin is an insult to the divine majesty, the equivalent of giving two fingers to the Queen. It is for this reason that sins that seem relatively trivial or inconsequential to us, for example Sabbath-breaking or gossip, are treated with the utmost seriousness in the Bible.[39]

Sin is a deviation from the norms established by God in creation, such that the greater the degree of divergence from the norm the greater the moral outrage the Bible expresses. It is for this reason that homosexual relationships between consenting adults are stigmatized as an 'abomination' in the Old Testament, even though they cause no harm to any third party. They are a greater deviation from the creation norm of heterosexual marriage as the only appropriate context for sexual relationships than, for example, polygamy or adultery.[40]

We need to allow God to determine the seriousness of sin for us, not our culture or our own feelings. Our tendency will always be to downplay the seriousness of the sins that we are prone to, in contrast to the sins we see others committing. Just as we foster our love and fear for God by mediating on who He is and what He has done, we ought to meditate on the numerous 'vice lists' in Scripture so as to cultivate a proper hatred of sin. Paul, for example, seeks to discourage the Christians in Corinth from sexual sin, and especially from making use of prostitutes, by reminding them of the reality of what this would mean:

> Do you not know that your bodies are members of Christ himself? Shall I then take the members of Christ and unite

---

38. See for example David in Psalm 51:4.
39. Exodus 31:14; Numbers 15:32-36; Romans 1:29.
40. Leviticus 18.

them with a prostitute? Never! Do you not know that he who unites himself with a prostitute is one with her in body? For it is said, 'The two will become one flesh.' But whoever is united with the Lord is one with him in Spirit ... Do you not know that your bodies are temples of the Holy Spirit, who is in you, whom you have received from God? You are not your own; you were bought at a price. Therefore honour God with your bodies.[41]

Alongside the hatred of sin, we need to have a proper hatred for Satan, who is the author of sin. The Bible tells us that he is a real spiritual enemy, not a mythological figure or still worse a figure of fun. He is the enemy of God and His kingdom, and aims to enslave and destroy. As Christians, we have been rescued from his kingdom and brought into the kingdom of God.[42] To fail to resist temptation is to conspire with the enemy and to work against God's purposes in the world. It is to serve as an enemy agent. We ought to recoil at the prospect of serving his purposes. Whilst Satan is a vicious enemy he is also a defeated enemy. If we belong to Christ he has no claim on us, and Jesus, who dwells in us by His spirit, is more powerful than him.[43] We are able to resist him, and when we do so he will flee from us.[44]

Whilst cultivating a deep and real hatred of sin and of Satan is essential and will provide some protection against the lure of temptation, it will not in itself be sufficient to enable us to mortify the desires of the flesh. However, if we take sin and Satan lightly we will not be willing to undertake the arduous

41. 1 Corinthians 6:15-20.
42. Colossians 1:13-14; Ephesians 2:1-10.
43. 1 John 4:4.
44. 1 Peter 5:8-9; James 4:7.

process of mortification as it will seem easier to capitulate than to fight.

Listen to God's Word

If the fight against temptation requires that we love and fear God, and hate sin and Satan, then it follows that we must listen to God's Word. Sinning is always an act of disobedience of God's commands, whether consciously or unconsciously. As we have seen, this was clearly the case in the Garden of Eden, when Adam and Eve ate the forbidden fruit, and at Mount Sinai where Israel made and worshipped the golden calf in contravention of the second commandment.

The Bible is not just a human book, but the living and active Word of God for His people.[45] The Scriptures were inspired by the Holy Spirit and they reveal God's plan of salvation accomplished in Jesus Christ and teach us how we ought to live as His people.[46] It is through the Bible that God reveals Himself to us, in His words and deeds. It is through the Bible that we come to know how loving and lovely God is, and how horrible sin is. We hear the unvarnished truth about ourselves and have the precious promises of salvation that bring us hope.

It follows that hearing God speak to us in the Bible is the best possible defence against temptation. If we read the Bible, and hear it faithfully preached and taught, we will develop a God-centred world view and an appropriate moral compass. We will no longer be taken in by the lies and deceit of our culture and will be able to make judgements about whether our desires are godly or wicked. This will enable us to identify temptations so that we can resist them.

---

45. Hebrews 4:12.
46. 2 Timothy 3:15-16.

So many of the temptations prevalent in our contemporary context arise because false teachers are distorting the Word of God and interpreting it to fit with their sinful desires. This is especially the case regarding issues of sex and sexuality. It is vital that we seek out faithful teachers, who expound and apply sound doctrine to our lives. Like the Bereans in Acts 17, we need to be carefully on our guard, and test whether what we are taught is true to the Scriptures.[47]

A good knowledge of the Scriptures will provide some measure of protection against temptation, ensuring that there are some desires that we dismiss immediately because we know them to be sinful. However, Scripture is also our primary defence against the temptations that do get a grip on us, and which must be countered if we are to resist them. The proper use of Scripture, which is the sword of the Spirit,[48] is one of the main means by which we mortify the desires of the flesh, so that we do not carry them into action. We need to argue with our temptations from Scripture, thus killing their plausibility and attractiveness, so that they no longer have any hold on us. Answering temptations with the truth of Scripture empties them of their power and their attraction, exposing them for the lies they really are.

This is exactly what Jesus did when He faced temptation in the wilderness at the start of His ministry.[49] As we noted earlier, Jesus faced direct temptation by Satan, who made false promises by distorting God's Word. Jesus countered each of the three temptations by quoting and applying apposite verses of Scripture.[50] These quotations undermined Satan's arguments

---

47. Acts 17:10-12.
48. Ephesians 6:17.
49. Matthew 4:1-11.
50. Deuteronomy 8:3; 6:16; 6:13.

and exposed the unimaginably serious consequences of disobedience. In a similar way Jesus countered the satanic temptation He faced through Peter, when he urged Him not to go the way of the cross, by reasserting the divine plan that He should fulfil the role of the Suffering Servant, as prophesied in the Scriptures.[51]

If we do not know the Scriptures we will not be able to tackle the temptations we experience in this way. We will be unable to cross-examine them and distinguish between truth and lies. The Word of God is the crucial offensive and defensive weapon against temptation. The daily discipline of reading God's Word for ourselves, and the weekly discipline of hearing it taught by faithful ministers in the local church, is a vital means of mortifying the desire of our flesh.

Pray for God's help

Watch and pray. This injunction from our Lord implies that we should maintain a clear, abiding apprehension of the great danger we face if we enter into temptation.

If one is always aware of the great danger, one will always stand guard. (John Owen)

> Have we trials and temptations?
> Is there trouble anywhere?
> We should never be discouraged,
> Take it to the Lord in prayer.
> Can we find a friend so faithful
> Who will all our sorrows share?
> Jesus knows our every weakness,
> Take it to the Lord in prayer.
> (Joseph Scriven, 'What a friend we have in Jesus')

---

51. Matthew 16:21-23; 17:11-12.

In the battle against temptation we need to listen to God speaking, but we also need to speak to God and plead for His help and power to resist. Prayer is the great privilege of Christians, who have come to know God as Father, and it is the prime means by which we express our utter dependence on Him. We can pray with confidence knowing that He is aware of our needs already, and that He will always answer our prayers according to His good purpose and loving character.

As is the case with the Word of God, prayer is both a protection against temptation and a weapon with which to fight temptation. Jesus taught us to pray to our Heavenly Father that He will not lead us into temptation,[52] and we can pray this with the confidence that He will not allow us to be tempted more than we can bear.[53] We can pray that He might keep us faithful until Jesus returns. We should pray that He will fill us with His Holy Spirit so that we are empowered to live a new life of obedience and godliness.

We must also turn to God in prayer for help when we face the immediate pressure of specific temptation. Once again this is the example that Jesus set for us in the Garden of Gethsemane, as He battled the temptation not to go to the cross and bear the wrath of God. He faced this intensely personal struggle by turning to His Father in prayer. Three times He devoted Himself to prayer, ultimately committing to obey His Father's will.

One striking feature of Jesus' praying in the Garden of Gethsemane is that He asked His closest disciples, Peter, James and John, to accompany Him, and to watch and pray with Him.[54] However, they fell asleep, leaving Him to pray

---

52. Matthew 6:13.
53. 1 Corinthians 10:13.
54. Matthew 26:36-44.

alone. He was surely seeking to teach them a lesson for the future, rebuking them and teaching them that the spirit is willing, but the flesh is weak.

It is difficult not to sense an echo of the struggle we experience between our fallen human flesh and the desires prompted by the Holy Spirit dwelling within us in these verses. This would suggest that mortification of the flesh by the Spirit does not occur automatically, but rather that we have to wrestle with God in prayer for the power of the Spirit to resist temptation. As Paul makes clear elsewhere, prayer is a crucial weapon in our spiritual warfare.[55] It is the Holy Spirit who prompts us to pray to our Father, and who prays for us when we do not know how to pray.[56] We cannot expect to enjoy victory in the fight against temptation and sin if we do not pray. Prayer is vital to killing temptation and mortifying the flesh.

The author of Hebrews also encourages his readers to pray for help when they are facing temptation. This was especially relevant because they were facing the threat of persecution and under pressure to abandon their faith in Christ and return to their former Judaism. He reminds them that the risen and ascended Lord Jesus is ministering as their great high priest at the right hand of God the Father. He is a 'merciful and faithful high priest'[57] who is 'able to help those who are being tempted' because He Himself suffered when He was tempted.[58] He therefore urges them to pray with confidence:

Therefore, since we have a great high priest who has ascended into heaven, Jesus the Son of God, let us hold firmly to the

---

55. Ephesians 6:18.
56. Romans 8:14-17; 26-27.
57. Hebrews 2:17.
58. Hebrews 2:18.

faith we profess. For we do not have a high priest who is unable to feel sympathy for our weaknesses, but we have one who has been tempted in every way, just as we are – yet he did not sin. Let us then approach God's throne of grace with confidence, so that we may receive mercy and find grace to help us in our time of need.[59]

We will only win our battle against temptation if we pray. It is for this reason that Paul prayed that God would give him the boldness to preach the gospel, since otherwise he might be tempted to remain silent for fear of persecution.[60] A person who is tempted to click and watch pornography online, to have one drink too many, to lie about their income on their tax return, or whatever other sin they might be contemplating, needs to pray for help and the power of the Spirit to overcome their weak flesh.

> Lord Jesus, hear my prayer,
> Your grace impart;
> when evil thoughts arise
> through Satan's art,
> O, drive them all away
> and do You, from day to day,
> keep me beneath Your sway,
> King of my heart.
> (E.T. Sibomana, 'O How the Grace of God Amazes Me')

FILL YOUR MIND WITH GOOD THOUGHTS
Temptations may be caused by external factors and stimuli, or arise from our fallen human flesh, but the battle against temptation is essentially fought in the mind. The mind is where we think tempting thoughts, and where we decide

---

59. Hebrews 4:14-16.
60. Ephesians 6:19-20; Colossians 4:2-4.

whether we are going to indulge them and act on them or resist them. It is no surprise that the transforming power of the gospel operates by renewing our minds and changing our thinking, so that we know what God's will is and find it to be good and pleasing.[61] The New Testament term for repentance literally means 'change of mind'. It is therefore essential that we use our minds in the right way and that we fill them with the right thoughts.

So much of our struggle with temptation occurs because we allow our minds to be filled with thoughts of sin. This is especially the case in a media and entertainment saturated culture, where virtually every film, television programme, book and advert is communicating a vision of sin that is attractive and fulfilling. If we allow such thoughts to dominate our thinking then it is not surprising that we experience greater temptation and find it much harder to resist our desires. Not only do we need to avoid filling our minds with those things that would encourage us to sin, and make sin attractive to us, but we need to ensure that our minds are occupied with alternative thoughts of what is good and holy.

Paul therefore urges the Christians in Philippi to make sure that they fill their minds with what is wholesome and good:

Finally, brothers and sisters, whatever is true, whatever is noble, whatever is right, whatever is pure, whatever is admirable – if anything is excellent or praiseworthy – think about such things. Whatever you have learned or received or heard from me, or seen in me – put it into practice. And the God of peace will be with you.[62]

---

61. Romans 12:1-2.
62. Philippians 4:8-9.

It would be wrong to reduce this principle to a set of legalistic rules about what we can or cannot watch, read or view, and we all have different personal levels of susceptibility to sin. Some of us may be more tempted by sexualized imagery, whereas others of us may be more tempted by lifestyle magazines that feed our covetousness for material possessions that connote style or success. However, we cannot expect to experience victory over temptation if we are blasé about what we fill our minds with.

Jesus' command to His disciples to take radical action against sin by plucking out their eye if it causes them to sin can be applied here. Mortifying the desires of the flesh may well mean refusing to watch or view that which would be unhelpful to our personal struggle against sin, and instead choosing to watch and read those things that would encourage good and godly thinking. We need to fuel our imagination with images and ideas that draw us towards obedience rather than disobedience, and with role models who make loving and serving God compelling and attractive.

Controlling the access of our minds to images and texts that prompt, promote and encourage sinful thought is especially important because these images and impressions lodge in our memories. They cannot be erased and may be a snare of temptation for years to come. For example, sexual images from decades ago can recur at moments of vulnerability and the battle has to be fought all over again. We need to do everything we can to avoid filling our memory banks with things that will provoke temptation. In effect, we download a vast quantity of sexualized imagery and pornography on to the hard-drive of our own memory, so that we no longer need to access the internet or other media because we can access our own mental library. It is better to avoid creating such memories in the first place.

Cultivate contentment

Much of the power of temptation to lead us into sin derives from the way that it plays on our insecurities and sense of dissatisfaction with our lives. We are vulnerable because we feel that we lack things that we either need or deserve, and which we are deceived into believing will bring us the happiness that we crave. This was certainly the case in the Garden of Eden, when Satan deceived Eve into thinking that God had withheld something good from her, that would enhance her life and experience, making her more competent and complete.[63] Much sexual temptation, for example, flows from a sense of dissatisfaction and discontent with our current sexual experience or lack thereof, whether within singleness or marriage. We are persuaded that sex with someone else will bring us the happiness and fulfilment we crave.

Paul very clearly links the power of temptation with discontent in his letter to Timothy, where he warns that:

> Those who want to get rich fall into temptation and a trap and into many foolish and harmful desires that plunge people into ruin and destruction. For the love of money is a root of all kinds of evil. Some people, eager for money, have wandered from the faith and pierced themselves with many griefs.[64]

To counter such temptations, it is essential to cultivate contentment and satisfaction with our current circumstances. We need to have faith that 'godliness with contentment is

---

63. Genesis 3:5.
64. 1 Timothy 6:9-10.

great gain.'[65] Paul was able to resist the temptation to exploit his ministry and status as an apostle for personal financial gain because he was content with the way that the Lord had provided for him and strengthened him. This contentment freed him to tell the Philippians that his needs had been amply supplied, so that they did not need to send him any more money:

> I have learned to be content whatever the circumstances. I know what it is to be in need, and I know what it is to have plenty. I have learned the secret of being content in any and every situation, whether well fed or hungry, whether living in plenty or in want. I can do all this through him who gives me strength.[66]

We learn this contentment by giving thanks for all the ways in which God has met our needs and provided for us, and by remembering that we came into the world with nothing and will take nothing out of it.[67] Even marriage is only for this world and will not last into the new creation.[68] We need to understand that God does not promise to meet our wants, but we can be sure that He will provide for our basic needs of food and clothing,[69] whether by providing work[70] or through the generosity of the Christian community.[71]

Western materialism and consumerism, which tempts us to try to do the impossible and serve both God and money, derives its power by confusing needs with wants, and fostering a sense of entitlement to more. We are unlikely

---

65. 1 Timothy 6:6.
66. Philippians 4:11-13.
67. 1 Timothy 6:6-8.
68. Matthew 22:30.
69. Matthew 6:25-34.
70. Ephesians 4:28; 2 Thessalonians 3:6-15.
71. Acts 4:32-35.

to learn the godly contentment that will protect us against temptation if we choose to spend our lives looking at adverts, reading lifestyle magazines or following the latest fashion vlogs.

Avoid tempting situations and individuals

Let us keep our spirits unentangled by avoiding all appearance of evil, and all the ways that lead there. Guard yourself especially in your social contacts and your occupations, which all contain pitfalls to entrap us. (John Owen)

Temptations can arise at any time from the desires of our fallen flesh, but it is often external stimuli that prompt our temptations. We are all unique individuals with different susceptibility to sin. We are attracted to different kinds of sin, and therefore more prone to temptation in these areas.

To use sexual temptations as a paradigm illustration, some people will be subject to heterosexual temptation, others to homosexual temptation, and others to both. We vary in who we find sexually attractive. There may be a particular kind of person, or a particular look, that we personally find more attractive than others, and which presents a greater danger. Encountering some people may therefore stir strong temptations, whereas encountering others may produce no temptation at all. We may be immediately physically attracted to some people, even though we do not know them at all, whereas in other cases we find that the closer we get to a person the more tempted we become.

If we are to resist temptation we need to know ourselves, so that we are aware of our specific vulnerabilities, and then take action to try to avoid situations and circumstances where we know that we might be unable to resist temptation.

In many cases it may well be that the 'way out' that God has provided is to avoid the tempting situation altogether.

As was mentioned above, for the Corinthians this meant that they could not attend the idol feasts at the pagan temples, even though they knew theologically that idols were nothing, and that these were important social and economic gatherings.[72] The Corinthians could not hope to resist the temptations of idolatry and sexual immorality if they were to frequent the temples where this was practised. It would be like a gambling addict attending a casino or an alcoholic going into a bar.

Mortification of our fallen flesh will therefore require avoiding those situations and circumstances which will cause us to be tempted. A good example of such proactive resistance can in found in the life of Joseph. While he was a trusted slave in the household of Potiphar he found himself the object of the sexual advances of Potiphar's wife, who wanted to go to bed with him. She pressured him day after day. Joseph's response to this repeated sexual invitation was not just to refuse to go to bed with her, but also to refuse, as far as it was possible for him, to 'even be with her.'[73] He protected himself as far as he could by avoiding the situation in which he would be most vulnerable. In the same way Daniel protected himself from compromising his Jewish identity and becoming beholden to King Nebuchadnezzar at the Babylonian court by refusing to eat the food from the king's table and instead eating only kosher vegetables.[74]

Very often the way in which we avoid temptation is by focusing on fulfilling our normal obligations in life. God has

---

72. 1 Corinthians 10:14-22.
73. Genesis 39:10.
74. Daniel 1:1-21.

given us responsibilities at work, home, family and as citizens, and this ought to keep us adequately occupied. In contrast distraction and idleness are an invitation to temptation. It is not surprising that David yielded to temptation and committed adultery with Bathsheba when he stayed at home in Jerusalem rather than leading his men in battle. 2 Samuel 11:1 pointedly tells us that:

> In the spring, at the time when kings go off to war, David sent
> Joab out with the king's men and the whole Israelite army.

David should have been at the front with his men, rather than on the roof watching a beautiful woman bathing. Of course, when he saw Bathsheba he should have averted his eyes rather than lingering and sending someone to find out who she was, but the initial step in his failure was that he was not where he was meant to have been.

Sometimes avoiding temptation means changing our life situation to reduce the opportunities and occasions for temptation. Paul offers very practical advice to the Christians in Corinth who were facing sexual temptation in a highly immoral culture, where it was quite usual and acceptable for men to satisfy their sexual lusts with slaves and prostitutes. Whilst he advocated the advantages of singleness as against marriage, he also knew that the celibacy that this would entail would be a burden that some would not be able to endure. He therefore advised those who could not maintain sexual continence to marry:

> Now to the unmarried and the widows I say: It is good for
> them to stay unmarried, as I do. But if they cannot control

themselves, they should marry, for it is better to marry than to burn with passion.[75]

Those who are married are not to abstain from their sexual relations, so as to protect one another from temptation.[76] It is likely that he gives very similar advice to the Thessalonian Christians, encouraging them to avoid sexual immorality by acquiring a wife.[77] Paul knows full well that this is not an answer for everyone, and that it is not a complete answer for anyone. But it is part of the answer for some who are struggling with sexual temptation. The 'way out' that God has provided for them is to marry and enjoy the blessing of sex in the proper context of heterosexual marriage.

Given that we are all different, the application of this principle cannot be distilled down to legalistic rules that apply universally to all Christians. We are all subject to temptation in general but are susceptible to different specific temptations. The temptations that we find most powerful and alluring may well change at different stages of our lives. There are characteristic sins and temptations of youth,[78] and different sins and temptations of old age. Men and women are often tempted in different ways, with men more susceptible to visual temptation and women more susceptible to relational temptation. We need to identify the boundaries that are appropriate for ourselves and our own predilections and vulnerabilities. We need to know the areas in life in which we are 'weak' and those where we are 'strong'.

Once again sexual temptation provides a paradigm example. For some men it may well be wise and necessary

---

75. 1 Corinthians 7:8-9.
76. 1 Corinthians 7:1-7.
77. 1 Thessalonians 4:3-4 (alternative translation in footnote).
78. 2 Timothy 2:22.

that they avoid spending time alone with a woman who is not their wife. However, for a person who struggles with same-sex attraction the very worst thing might be to spend time alone with other men. Whereas it might be unwise for a single man wishing to avoid sexual immorality to go on holiday with a single girl, it may be equally unwise for a same-sex attracted man to go on holiday with another man, and perfectly safe to go on holiday with a girl. The same would go for having dinner together or sharing a car without other passengers.

Some people who struggle with viewing internet pornography will be adequately protected if they install filters and accountability software on their computers, or if they only ever use a computer in a public place. Others may struggle to such an extent that they must renounce the ownership and use of any devices that have access to the internet. Some people have the resilience to go to a bar with their work colleagues after work, whereas others know that they would be unable to resist the temptation to drink to excess because of the social pressure and desire to be accepted.

It is not only necessary to avoid specific situations, but it may be necessary to avoid close contact with specific individuals who might lead us into temptation, and where developing a close relationship would make it harder to resist sinful desires. Paul makes it very clear to the Corinthians that they are not required to avoid social contact with everyone who is an unbeliever and sexually immoral, since this would require them to leave the world altogether, which is impossible.[79] However, he did command them to separate themselves completely from professing Christians who had committed sexual immorality and were subject to church

---

79. 1 Corinthians 5:9-10.

discipline because they remained unrepentant for their sin.[80] This radical action was required to protect the church and ensure that others were not led into the same sin,[81] as well as to try to save the sinner by bringing him to repentance and renewed faith.

In the same way Christians are commanded to have nothing to do with false teachers who will undermine their faith in Christ, and to avoid entering into business partnerships with pagans, as this will potentially tempt them to idolatry by participating in the temple worship that was the prerequisite of most economic and trade activity in the ancient world.[82]

The book of Proverbs similarly warns God's people to avoid unhelpful friendships that might lead them into sin, and the opening chapters advocate the pursuit of wisdom, which starts with the fear of God, using the metaphor of a father urging his youthful son to keep away from the adulterous woman and resist her seductions. Psalm 1 likewise highlights the way that the 'righteous man' avoids associating with those who could lead him astray from delight in the Word of God:

> Blessed is the one
> who does not walk in step with the wicked
> or stand in the way that sinners take
> or sit in the company of mockers.[83]

One of the most common examples of the need to separate from individuals who might lead God's people into sin, becoming a source of temptation for them, are the repeated commands and warnings not to marry outside of the people

---

80. 1 Corinthians 5:11.
81. 1 Corinthians 5:6-8.
82. 2 Corinthians 6:14-18.
83. Psalm 1:1.

of God. God commands the Israelites not to marry their sons or daughters to the Canaanite or other pagan people,[84] a command that they repeatedly disobey with disastrous consequences. Solomon is led into wicked apostasy and the worship of foreign gods by his many foreign wives.[85] Even after the return from exile such mixed marriages provide a fertile ground for temptation. [86] The New Testament echoes these commands, though with a new-covenant perspective in which faith has taken the place of race as the crucial criteria. Paul thus instructs widows in Corinth that, if they choose to marry, their intended spouse 'must belong to the Lord.'[87] Whilst those who are married to an unbeliever when they are converted are not required to separate from their spouse because of their new spiritual incompatibility, those who are free to choose should not put themselves into a situation where they might be tempted to compromise their loyalty to Christ. The refusal to marry an unbeliever, or to have close friendships and partnership with those who would exacerbate temptation, is therefore an example of the costly radical action that is needed to mortify the flesh.

Mortification will mean different radical action for different Christians. It is for this reason that we need to be careful not to judge brothers and sisters who make different choices and draw their boundaries in different places. The crucial question is whether the choices they make enable them to fight sin and resist temptation, or whether they cause them to fall into sin.

---

84. Deuteronomy 7:3.
85. 1 Kings 11:1-12.
86. Ezra 9-10.
87. 1 Corinthians 7:39.

AVOID THINGS THAT REDUCE YOUR ABILITY TO EXERCISE SELF-CONTROL

As we have seen, the fight against temptation and sin requires us to take radical action in our lives. Our sanctification requires active cooperation with the work of God by the Holy Spirit. It is not surprising that the New Testament therefore puts a great deal of stress on our need to be sober so that we can exercise self-control. Fighting temptation requires us to be clear-headed, quick thinking and ruthlessly decisive. We need to avoid anything that causes us to lose the mental agility and sharpness essential for this battle. Whilst the Bible regards wine as a blessing from God, and does not command total abstinence, it warns against intoxication and drunkenness because they lower our defences against temptation. Those who have drunk too much alcohol will be less willing and able to fight against sin, in just the same way that a soldier on watch will be unable to respond to the surprise attack of the enemy if he is drunk at his post. What is true of alcohol is equally true of drugs that dull the senses and lower our inhibitions.

Our defences against temptation will also be lowered when we are tired, as we will lack the mental sharpness that we need. Many Christians fall prey to temptation because they have overworked and exhausted themselves and failed to maintain a proper pattern of work and rest. Irrespective of whether we believe that the Sabbath command remains applicable to new covenant believers, the pattern of work and rest is embedded in creation and ignored at our peril. Failure to get proper refreshing sleep will leave us vulnerable and less able to say 'No!' to temptation and mortify sinful desires before we act on them.

We need to respect our physical limitations and take proper care of our bodies so that we are fighting fit for the battle. Sensible routines of work and rest are a prerequisite to resistance. In a fallen world there will inevitably be times when we are physically more vulnerable, perhaps because of illness or the demands of a new baby leading to sleep deprivation. Whilst we must do all that we can to mitigate the impact of such life stages, we need to be aware of the greater vulnerability that they create, and so need to take greater care to protect ourselves. We may need to avoid situations and individuals that would ordinarily be unproblematic for us, because we know that our defences are down, and we have less capability to resist. For example, a business trip with a colleague might ordinarily present no difficulty, but if we are ill, depressed, stressed or know that our work will render us exhaustingly tired, we will need to take greater care and different action.

FLEE FROM TEMPTATION

Whilst we ought to take preventative steps to avoid temptation, the fact that we live in a fallen world and remain in our fallen human flesh means that there are bound to be circumstances in which we unexpectedly encounter temptation. We had not been expecting it, but we find that we are facing a moment of choice as to whether we fall into sin. It may be that we are watching a film or a programme and we had not anticipated the steamy sex scene that tempts us to lust. It may be that the conversation with our work colleagues takes an unexpected turn, and they are suggesting that we take the client to the lap-dancing bar to celebrate the deal. It may be that a person we thought was just a friend begins to proposition us and makes clear that they would be open to a sexual encounter. It may be that we are driving along the street and there is a prostitute soliciting on the side of the road, or a massage parlour amongst the shops.

When we are confronted with direct and forceful temptation in these ways the way out is quite simply to flee from the situation or the person concerned. Flight rather than fight might be the only way to resist the temptation, and this is what mortification will require. Flight may well be socially embarrassing and awkward, but that is the necessary cost of remaining faithful to God.

The New Testament repeatedly urges Christians to flee from temptation, and again sexual temptation is the paradigm. Paul urged the Corinthian Christians to 'flee from sexual immorality'[88] and to 'flee from idolatry'.[89] He commanded Timothy to flee from the love of money[90] and to 'flee the evil desires of youth'.[91]

Joseph provides us with a classic example of what such flight might involve. Although, as we have seen, he sought to avoid ever being with Potiphar's wife, on one occasion she caught him unawares in the house. Joseph's response was to run from the situation:

> One day he went into the house to attend to his duties, and none of the household servants was inside. She caught him by his cloak and said, 'Come to bed with me!' But he left his cloak in her hand and ran out of the house.[92]

WAGING TOTAL WAR

The battle we face against temptation and sin is lifelong and fierce. However, as we have seen, it is not an impossible fight

---

88. 1 Corinthians 6:18. See also 1 Thessalonians 4:3.
89. 1 Corinthians 10:14.
90. 1 Timothy 6:10-11.
91. 2 Timothy 2:22.
92. Genesis 39:11-12.

that we are destined to lose. We are not called to make a heroic last stand, but rather to stand firm and triumph over our enemies in the power of Christ. The fight will take many forms, and there is no single weapon that will enable us to win it. God supplies us with all the weapons that we need to win this war, but we need to be adaptable and utilize the right weapon and the right tactics for each situation. The war will not be won by rigid legalistic formulas, but by understanding ourselves and our enemy, and fighting 'smart'. Above all we need to be wholeheartedly committed to the fight, prepared to use every available strategy and every available weapon, so as to prevail. God always provides us with a way out from temptation, and we have to be determined to take it.

5

WHAT SHOULD WE DO WHEN WE SIN?

Before the throne of God above
I have a strong, a perfect plea;
A great high priest whose name is love,
Who ever lives and pleads for me.
My name is graven on his hands,
My name is written on his heart;
I know that while in heaven he stands
no tongue can bid me thence depart,
no tongue can bid me thence depart.
(Charitie L. Bancroft, 'Before the Throne of God Above')

The burden of this book has been to encourage Christians that, whilst temptation is an inevitable experience because they remain in their fallen human flesh, they can fight against it and, by the power of the Holy Spirit, live a victorious life. They are not condemned to a futile struggle and inevitable despair. We can mortify the sinful desires of the flesh and use our bodies in the service of righteousness.

However, even though the normal Christian life is not the pattern of failure and despair described in Romans 7, our mortification is never perfect in this life. We give in to temptation, with the result that we do not love God, neighbours or enemies as we should. Sometimes we sin in ways that are secret and unnoticed, at other times we sin in public ways that bring discredit to the gospel and call into question the reality of our profession of faith. Given that we do fall into sin, we need to ask what we should do when we fail to enjoy the victory that Christ has won for us, and to which we are entitled by our union with Him in His death and resurrection.

The Bible is a great help to us because it provides many examples of God's regenerate people falling into sin when they failed to resist temptation. Rather than forfeiting their salvation they turned to God in repentance and faith, and in return experienced His mercy and restoration. We read of how David was forgiven after his adultery with Bathsheba and murder of Uriah,[1] and of how Peter was forgiven and restored after he succumbed to pressure and denied Jesus three times.[2] The way that God dealt with their failures shows us that there can be mercy for us when we fall and fail. The New Testament letters also encourage us that mercy and forgiveness are available through Jesus if we repent and confess our sins.

OUR SIN DOES NOT INVALIDATE OUR JUSTIFICATION

When we fall into sin we need to remember that our failure does not automatically invalidate our justification. When we put our faith in Christ for the first time we were justified

---

1. 2 Samuel 12:13; Psalm 51.
2. John 21:15-19.

by God and declared to be righteous before Him. God pronounced this verdict on us because Jesus had already made a perfect sacrifice for our sins, satisfying the justice of God and removing His wrath from us. The perfect righteousness of Christ is counted to us because we have been united to Him by faith. Our sins have been forgiven and we are reconciled to God.

The sins we commit after we become Christians, when we have been regenerated and justified, do not remove the righteous status that we have been given. Our standing before God was not achieved by our performance, and it is not maintained by our performance. We are justified by faith from 'first to last'.[3] We are not saved by faith and then kept by our works.

A Christian who sins is not, therefore, recapitulating the fall of Genesis 3. We live the other side of the cross and resurrection. When Jesus died on the cross He paid the full penalty for all the sins that we would ever commit, not just the sins we had committed before we put our faith and trust in Him. Jesus' death operates outside of human time. When Jesus died He bore the just judgement of God for all the sins that all His people had committed until that time, and which had been left unpunished because the sacrifice of mere animals was purely symbolic rather than effective to remove sins.[4] Since God is omniscient and knows the future, Jesus also bore the full penalty for all the sins that would be committed by God's people after the historical moment of the cross. Jesus' death was a 'once for all' sacrifice for sins, that would never

---

3. Romans 1:17.
4. Romans 3:25.

have to be repeated.[5] This inevitably means that the cross dealt with not just past sins but also future sins.

It follows that God's people do not lose their justification when they yield to temptation and fall into sin. Abraham, for example, was justified when he trusted God's promise that he would have a son of his own flesh.[6] He did not lose his justification when he failed to trust God's promises and chose to have a son by Hagar, his wife's slave,[7] nor when he sought to save his own life by pretending that Sarah was his sister rather than his wife.[8]

We don't know the exact moment that David was justified,[9] though it was certainly at a very young age before he fought Goliath, but he did not lose his justification when he committed adultery with Bathsheba,[10] nor when he gave into temptation and sinned by undertaking a census of the fighting men in Israel.[11]

Peter was presumably justified when he professed his faith that Jesus was the Christ and the Son of God,[12] and he did not lose his justification when he denied Christ,[13] nor when he succumbed to the temptation of pressure in Antioch and sinned by refusing to eat with gentile Christians.[14]

Jesus Himself taught and demonstrated the difference between the definitive cleansing and forgiveness of sins that people receive when they first trust in Him and are born again,

---

5. Romans 6:10; Hebrews 7:27; 10:11-14.
6. Genesis 15:6; Romans 4:1-3.
7. Genesis 16.
8. Genesis 20:1-18.
9. Romans 4:6-9.
10. 2 Samuel 11.
11. 2 Samuel 24:1-17.
12. Matthew 16:16.
13. Matthew 26:69-75.
14. Galatians 2:11-21.

and the effects of their subsequent sinning, when He washed the feet of His disciples at the start of the Lord's Supper.[15] John tells us that Peter initially resisted having Jesus wash his feet, because he felt that it was unseemly for his lord to take the place of a servant. In their subsequent interchange Jesus draws the distinction between a person who needs a bath and someone who has dirty feet:

> He came to Simon Peter, who said to him, 'Lord, are you going to wash my feet?'
>
> Jesus replied, 'You do not realise now what I am doing, but later you will understand.'
>
> 'No,' said Peter, 'you shall never wash my feet.'
>
> Jesus answered, 'Unless I wash you, you have no part with me.'
>
> 'Then, Lord,' Simon Peter replied, 'not just my feet but my hands and my head as well!'
>
> Jesus answered, 'Those who have had a bath need only to wash their feet; their whole body is clean. And you are clean, though not every one of you.' For he knew who was going to betray him, and that was why he said not everyone was clean.[16]

Jesus was reassuring Peter, and His other disciples, that they had already been declared clean and did not need to be cleansed again. They did not need to be, as it were, reconverted and rebaptized every time that they sinned. They had trusted in the one who is 'the Lamb of God who takes away the sin of the world'.[17] They only required a minor washing away of the muck they had accumulated. In contrast Judas Iscariot was not clean, because he had never truly trusted in Jesus.

---

15. John 13:1-17.
16. John 13:6-11.
17. John 1:29.

We can take great encouragement from these verses and examples, which show that our justification is secure and settled the moment we trust in Christ. Justification is the declaration of the final verdict of acquittal, or innocence, on the last day brought into the present when we trust Christ. Our righteous status, which has been conferred by the imputation of His perfect righteousness, is not and cannot be lost because we fall into sin. God does not cease to be our loving Father, and He does not change His mind about the verdict He has declared on us. We do not need to be converted all over again. This great truth is the foundation for our assurance and confidence that we can come boldly to God for the mercy we need.

Whilst succumbing to temptation and sinning as a Christian does not automatically forfeit our justification and standing with God, it may call into question the reality of our profession and whether we were truly born again and justified in the first place. This will be revealed by the attitude we have to the sin we have committed and, in particular, by whether we repent and acknowledge the wickedness of what we have done. The failure to take our sin seriously, and to confess and repent, is a sure sign that we are not regenerate believers in the Lord Jesus, and that we need to be converted and come to true faith for the first time. It is not that we have lost our justification by our sin, but rather that our defiant and complacent attitude to our sin shows that we were never justified in the first place. The New Testament makes clear that there will be some people who profess faith and yet turn out never to have been true believers. Such people fail to endure, and they die without maintaining a personal trust in Jesus as their Lord and Saviour.[18]

Our sin will impair our relationship with God

Whilst we will not lose our justification if we succumb to temptation and sin as Christians, this does not mean that there will be no impact on our relationship with God. Our fellowship and communion with God will be impaired by our sin, and we will not enjoy the joyful intimacy that we ought to experience. God may withhold His blessings from us and may exercise His loving discipline towards us to train us in righteousness.

On the one hand, our fellowship with God will be impaired because our sin has offended Him and attracted His displeasure. It may cause Him to turn His face from us, and no longer be attentive to us as He once was. He may no longer bless our work and ministry in the way He once did. On the other hand, the guilt and shame that we feel about our sin, and a sense of feeling dirty or unclean, may make us feel that we cannot come into the presence of God because of His purity and holiness. The sin of believers will not reverse their justification, but it may well have relational, psychological and even physical consequences.

This was certainly the experience of David when he fell into sin. When he had sinned, he knew that he needed to be cleansed in order to enjoy restored fellowship and intimacy with God.[19] He knew that God's hand was heavy on him because he had sinned,[20] but he was also weighed down by his

---

18. See for example Jesus' Parable of the Sower in Mark 4:1-20.
19. See for example Psalms 32 and 51.
20. Psalm 32:4.

own guilt and shame because of his wrongdoing.[21] The result of his sin was not that he had lost his salvation, but that he had lost the joy of his salvation, and longed for it to be restored.[22] He therefore cried out to God for mercy, forgiveness and cleansing.

The need for cleansing to restore relational intimacy with God and the joy of salvation seems to be what Jesus meant when He told Peter that those who have had a bath need only to wash their feet. Sin defiles us and impairs our relationship with God, but our relationship will be restored if we repent and seek His mercy.

WHEN WE SIN WE SHOULD CONFESS AND REPENT

> Depth of mercy! Can there be
> mercy still reserved for me?
> Can my God his wrath forbear?
> me, the chief of sinners, spare?
>
> Now Lord, move me to repent,
> let me now my sin lament;
> now my proud revolt deplore,
> weep, believe and sin no more.
> (Charles Wesley, 'Depth of Mercy')

When we sin as Christians, because we have yielded to temptation, we need to seek cleansing to restore our fellowship with God and the joy of our salvation. Our status has not changed but we do not enjoy the full blessings of our secure status as we should. The way that we regain an unimpaired and intimate relationship with God is by confession and repentance. We must acknowledge our sins before God and

---

21. Psalm 51:3-4.
22. Psalm 51:12.

turn from them and towards Him in humble contrition and faith. What God desires is not another sacrifice to cover our sins,[23] nor that we seek to regain His approval by our good works. The once-for-all propitiatory sacrifice of Christ for our sins is the only sacrifice that we need, and it remains fully effective to remove our sin.[24] Rather He responds in love and grace to a 'broken spirit' which is a 'broken and contrite heart'.[25] We need to appropriate the sacrifice that has already been made by renewed faith, so that we experience its effects. It is not sufficient that we are sorry for our failure. Our sorrow must lead us to seek transformation and resolve to live differently in the future.

The process of cleansing and restoration when we have fallen into sin is most fully explained by the apostle John in his first letter. He writes:

> If we claim to be without sin, we deceive ourselves and the truth is not in us. If we confess our sins, he is faithful and just and will forgive us our sins and purify us from all unrighteousness. If we claim we have not sinned, we make him out to be a liar and his word is not in us.
>
> My dear children, I write this to you so that you will not sin. But if anybody does sin, we have an advocate with the Father – Jesus Christ, the Righteous One. He is the atoning sacrifice for our sins, and not only for ours but also for the sins of the whole world.[26]

John makes clear that Christians who have sinned can be confident that Jesus' once-for-all sacrifice is sufficient to

---

23. Psalm 51:16.
24. 1 John 2:2.
25. Psalm 51:17.
26. 1 John 1:8-2:2.

forgive and purify them, and that this forgiveness is accessed by confessing our sins to Him.

Confession means admitting and acknowledging that we have sinned, and that we stand in need of forgiveness and cleansing. It is the very opposite of covering up what we have done, or of making excuses for our sin and trying to pass the blame to others. Confession is accepting the truth about ourselves and our actions, equivalent to owning up to the wrong we have done.

This is exactly what we see David doing in the Old Testament when he had fallen into sin. In Psalm 32 he contrasts his experience before and after he had confessed his sin:

> When I kept silent,
> My bones wasted away
> through my groaning all day long.
> For day and night
> your hand was heavy on me;
> my strength was sapped
> as in the heat of summer.
>
> Then I acknowledged my sin to you
> and did not cover up my iniquity.
> I said, 'I will confess
> my transgressions to the LORD.'
> And you forgave
> the guilt of my sin.[27]

David's confession led to him enjoying the blessing of forgiveness and removal of his sins.[28]

---

27. Psalm 32:3-5.
28. Psalm 32:1-2.

We see a similar confession of sins in Psalm 51, when David seeks God's forgiveness, cleansing and restoration after his adultery with Bathsheba. At first, he had supressed the wickedness of his sin, and refused to acknowledge it. However, after he was confronted and convicted by the Word of God through the prophet Nathan he immediately acknowledged his sin and accepted his guilt before God.[29] In Psalm 51 David acknowledges the wickedness of his sin and justice of God:

> For I know my transgressions,
> and my sin is always before me.
> Against you, you only, have I sinned
> and done what is evil in your sight;
> so you are right in your verdict
> and justified when you judge.[30]

Sometimes it will be appropriate to confess our sins to fellow believers,[31] but it is always necessary to confess them to God to access His ongoing mercy. This is also reflected in the Lord's Prayer, in which Jesus taught His disciples to pray:

> Forgive us our sins,
> for we also forgive everyone who sins against us.[32]

Confessing our sins is not just a mechanical or intellectual exercise but must flow from a true grasp of the seriousness and wickedness of our sins. They are an affront to God. Confession is thus an aspect of repentance, which means turning away from our sins and turning instead to obedience to God. Our confession will be empty if it seeks forgiveness and cleansing without any desire to change and live differently in the future.

---

29. 2 Samuel 12:13.
30. Psalm 51:3-4.
31. James 5:16.
32. Luke 11:4.

True repentance is evidenced by godly sorrow for sin that leads to a change in life and behaviour. This is different from a mere sorrow at having fallen into sin, which is essentially a frustration with ourselves, and our personal failure and the shame it brings, rather than a real desire to live a new life.[33] In the two Psalms quoted above, David not only acknowledged his sin to God, but also expressed his resolve to live differently in the future,[34] including teaching others to live in obedience to God.

The difference between true repentance and apparent repentance is well illustrated by the contrast between the ways Peter and Judas Iscariot responded to their sin of rejecting Jesus. Both bitterly regretted their actions the night that Jesus was arrested, but only Peter truly repented. Judas regretted that he had betrayed Jesus to the Jewish authorities and was so emotionally overwhelmed that he returned the money he had received and committed suicide.[35] He did not, however, turn back to Jesus and seek His mercy. He chose to continue to reject Jesus and to bear the just punishment for his sin himself. Peter was deeply grieved that he had disowned Jesus, and 'wept bitterly'[36] because of what he had done. He turned back to Jesus and was ultimately reconciled to Him and restored to his ministry.[37]

The willingness to confess and repent is the evidence that demonstrates that a person is a true believer in Christ, who has been regenerated and justified. Our new life in Christ begins with repentance and continues to be a life of ongoing repentance. However, a person who falls into sin and refuses

---

33. 2 Corinthians 7:2-13.
34. Psalm 32:8-9; Psalm 51:13.
35. Matthew 27:1-10.
36. Matthew 26:75.
37. John 21:15-19.

to repent demonstrates that they were never a believer in the first place.

This is seen in the contrast between King David and King Saul. Both professed to have faith in God, and both fell into temptation and committed serious sins. David committed adultery with Bathsheba and conducted a prideful census of his fighting men.[38] Saul took it upon himself to offer sacrifices to God rather than wait for Samuel the priest to arrive,[39] and failed to obey God's command to put to death all the animals when he defeated the Amalekites.[40] Whereas David immediately confessed and repented when he was confronted with the truth about his sin,[41] Saul responded by seeking to make excuses for his sin and justifying his own actions.[42] Whilst David's sin might seem to have been much more serious, and Saul's somewhat trivial in comparison, their different responses revealed that David was 'a man after God's own heart', whereas Saul was not.

The encouraging lesson for us is that it is not the fact that we succumb to temptation and fall into sin that casts doubt on our faith in Christ. Provided we confess and repent with true godly sorrow, accompanied by an honest resolve to live differently in the future, we are showing that our faith is genuine. However, if we refuse to confess and repent we confirm that our profession of faith is false and that we are not truly born again and justified. We need to be saved.

The availability of forgiveness for the sin of believers is also embedded in the process of church discipline, which is designed to deal with professing Christians who fall

---

38. 2 Samuel 11 and 2 Samuel 24.
39. 1 Samuel 13:1-15.
40. 1 Samuel 15:1-35.
41. 2 Samuel 12:13.
42. 1 Samuel 13:11-12; 15:20-21.

into sin and refuse to repent. Church discipline is much misunderstood, and it is not intended as a way of punishing Christians who have fallen into sin.[43] Rather it is a process for discerning whether those who have fallen into open sin are truly believers.

Paul explains the proper use of church discipline to the church in Corinth, where one of the members of the church had committed sexual immorality by sleeping with his father's wife.[44] The crucial element that made church discipline essential in that instance was that the individual concerned was not repentant for what he had done, but proud of his actions. Paul therefore instructed the church that they were to excommunicate him, which means that they were to put him out of the fellowship of the church and treat him as an unbeliever. In so doing they were following the commands Jesus gave on how to deal with sin in the church.[45]

Paul's motivation for this apparently extreme action was to protect the church, but also to bring the man to repentance so that he might be saved.[46] Church discipline would bring home to him the true seriousness of his sin and prevent him from enjoying a false assurance that he was a Christian. This process, painful as it must have been, ultimately had its desired effect. In 2 Corinthians Paul wrote to the church again to urge them to welcome back into the fellowship a sinner who had repented.[47] The process of church discipline, and the repentance it produced, had shown that he was a true

---

43. On occasions God may do this directly, as for example, in 1 Corinthians 11:27-32; Acts 5:1-11 and possibly James 5:13-16.
44. 1 Corinthians 5:1-5.
45. Matthew 18:15-20.
46. 1 Corinthians 5:5.
47. 2 Corinthians 2:5-11.

believer, that he had been forgiven by God, and so he ought to be accepted by the church.

In an indirect way, the New Testament teaching about church discipline thus brings reassurance and comfort to Christians who have yielded to temptation and fallen into sin. If they are genuinely repentant for what they have done, then they do not need to be subjected to church discipline. Their sin has already been dealt with by their repentance and confession. They have been cleansed and their full fellowship with God restored and renewed. Therefore, they can enjoy full fellowship with the other members of the church. Confession and repentance ought to be the norm for Christians, whereas church discipline is an exceptional measure that will expose that a professing believer is not a real Christian at all.

Trust God's promise of forgiveness and restoration

O Jesus, full of truth and grace
More full of grace than I of sin;
I now would flee to thine embrace;
Open thine arms and take me in,
And freely my backslidings heal,
And love the faithless sinner still.

Thou know'st the way to bring me back,
My fallen spirit to restore;
O for Thy truth and mercy's sake,
Forgive, and bid me sin no more;
The ruins of my soul repair,
And make my heart a house of prayer.

The stone to flesh do thou convert;
And all my guilt and sin remove;

Sprinkle thy blood upon my heart,
And melt it by thy dying love;
This rebel heart by love subdue,
And make it soft, and make it new.

O, give me, Lord, the tender heart,
That trembles at the approach of sin;
A godly fear of sin impart;
Implant and root it deep within,
That I may dread Thy gracious power,
And never dare to offend Thee more.
(Charles Wesley, 'O Jesus, Full of Truth and Grace')

Christians who have fallen into temptation and sin, but who have confessed and repented, can be assured that God has forgiven, cleansed and restored them. Their sin had already been dealt with by the death of Christ, and they enjoy the benefits of the atonement He has made. This is nothing less than the promise of God, and we are called to take Him at His Word.

The passage we quoted from 1 John above assures us that if we confess our sins to God 'he is faithful and just and will forgive us our sins and purify us from all unrighteousness.'[48] The risen Lord Jesus has ascended to the right hand of God in heaven, where He continues to minister as our high priest and advocate, pleading the efficacy of His atoning death on our behalf to His Father. Jesus' sacrificial work has been completed, but His intercessory work on our behalf continues, ensuring that we receive ongoing forgiveness and cleansing.[49] There is no additional sacrifice necessary, but there is a need to keep applying the benefits of the sacrifice that has been made.

---

48. 1 John 1:9.
49. Hebrews 7:25.

David experienced the fulfilment of this promise when he repented and confessed his sin with Bathsheba. His sin was forgiven, his guilt removed, and his relationship with God restored, as he testifies so eloquently in Psalm 51. The Holy Spirit was not taken from him, as it had been from Saul, and he was not cast from God's presence or the kingship. Peter experienced the fulfilment of this promise when he was restored by the Lord Jesus after the resurrection.[50] In a very deliberate echo of Peter's threefold denial, three times Jesus asked him to confess his love for Him, and then reinstated him to his ministry amongst the disciples and the church. The sinner in Corinth who was subjected to church discipline evidently repented and experienced the forgiveness of Christ, Paul and the church.[51]

However, lest it be thought that there is cheap grace when Christians fall into temptation and sin, the forgiveness that is promised if we confess our sins does not guarantee that there will be no consequences for our sin. Forgiveness does not undo all the results of our actions. For example, even though David was fully forgiven for his adultery with Bathsheba, the child that was conceived in their sin died, and his family was subjected to rebellion and civil war.[52] David did not lose his throne, but his kingdom did forfeit the peace and unity that it had enjoyed until that time.

Some sins have consequences for Christian service that cannot be undone by confession and repentance. A pastor who commits adultery can be forgiven for his sin by God, but he will be disqualified from the ministry because he no longer

---

50. John 21:15-19.
51. 2 Corinthians 2:5-11.
52. 2 Samuel 12:7-14.

meets the biblical criteria for church leadership.[53] The same goes for those who succumb to the temptation to financial dishonesty or drunkenness. Their relationship with God may be restored, but they cannot continue in leadership of His people.

We are reassured by God's Word that there is no sin that is so serious that it cannot be forgiven. Paul recalls how he was the 'chief of sinners' because he persecuted the church, and yet he received God's mercy and forgiveness.[54] Moses and David, along with Paul, were both murderers. David was an adulterer. The Corinthian Christians had been guilty of a catalogue of vile sins.[55] In the final analysis Christians are all wicked sinners who have received mercy, because 'there is no one righteous, not even one.'[56] The sobering truth is that 'all have sinned and fall short of the glory of God.'[57] Jesus did not come into the world to condemn sinners, but to save sinners.[58]

We need to understand and believe that the only sin that cannot be forgiven is the sin of unbelief. The refusal to believe that Jesus is the Christ and the Son of God, that He is Lord and has risen from the dead, is the unforgivable sin of 'blasphemy against the Holy Spirit'.[59] This is the reason that there can be no hope of salvation for those who have apostatized and abandoned their former faith in Christ.[60]

If we are Christians, we will face a lifetime battling against temptation. Though we will enjoy many victories by the

---

53. 1 Timothy 3:1-7; Titus 1:6-9.
54. 1 Timothy 1:15-16.
55. 1 Corinthians 6:9-11.
56. Romans 3:10.
57. Romans 3:23.
58. 1 Timothy 1:15.
59. Mark 3:28-9.
60. Hebrews 6:4-8.

power of the Spirit, there will be times when we fail to mortify our flesh and fall into sin. However, Christ will not abandon us. He knew what we were like when He chose us in eternity, and He paid for all the sins we would ever commit when He died on the cross. If we repent and confess our sins, and keep trusting Him as our Lord and Saviour, He will bring us safely into eternal glory and the new creation, where we will be with Him forever and finally free of temptation and sin.

Establish a loving community of mutual forgiveness

Whilst Christians who yield to temptation and fall into sin can be assured that they will experience God's forgiveness if they turn to Him in confession and repentance, sadly they may not experience the same grace and forgiveness from fellow believers. Individuals they have directly hurt or offended may refuse to forgive them, and the wider community of the church may refuse to accept them. The fear of lack of forgiveness from fellow believers, and the social ostracism and shame that admitting to sin may bring, is one of the main reasons we find it hard to be honest about our temptations and our sins. Bitter experience has taught us that our brothers and sisters in Christ may not be as gracious and merciful as our Heavenly Father.

Christians are not saved just for a private personal relationship with God, but are saved into the community of the church, which is the body of Christ. We are adopted by God and gain a whole family of brothers and sisters in Christ. Our churches are meant to be places of acceptance and mutual forgiveness. We stand together as sinners who have repented and received God's underserved mercy, and we are called to forgive one another just as we have been forgiven. We have no grounds to think ourselves superior to other brothers and sisters in Christ, even if they have fallen into sin in more spectacular and obvious ways than us.

As members of the church we are called to support and encourage one another, helping each other to resist temptation. When we fall into sin, and genuinely repent, we are to be as quick to forgive as God Himself. Jesus made this clear in His teaching. The Lord's Prayer, which is the family prayer He modelled to His disciples, links the forgiveness we receive from God with the forgiveness that we must offer one another:

> Forgive us our sins,
> for we also forgive everyone who sins against us.[61]

This prayer does not base our forgiveness on the fact that we have forgiven others, but it does insist that we can only come to God to ask for the forgiveness that we need if we are also willing to extend that forgiveness to our fellow believers.

Jesus' parable of the unmerciful servant[62] likewise teaches that if we have received God's mercy then we must practise mercy towards our brothers and sisters in Christ. We have each been forgiven an incalculable debt by God, which symbolizes the just punishment our sins deserve, which we could never possibly repay. How then can we refuse to forgive the comparatively trivial debts that we owe to one another? If we refuse to forgive our fellow believers then we show that we do not really belong to the kingdom of God at all, and we will rightly be excluded from it.

The New Testament therefore teaches that Christians are to practise mutual forgiveness within the family of the church.

---

61. Luke 11:4.
62. Matthew 18:21-35.

As Paul writes to the Colossians, we are to 'forgive as the Lord forgave you.'[63] We are to be kind and compassionate to one another, 'forgiving each other, just as in Christ God forgave you.'[64] We have no right to judge fellow believers who have been forgiven and accepted by the Lord Jesus. He is their master, and they are accountable to Him.[65] It is not our place to question the master's forgiveness.

It is for this reason, as we saw above, that Paul urged the Corinthians to forgive and accept the man who had sinned, and who most likely had been subjected to church discipline after they had received his first letter. He had caused great grief both to the congregation and to Paul, but they now needed to practise forgiveness because he had shown true godly sorrow. Paul wrote:

> The punishment inflicted on him by the majority is sufficient. Now instead, you ought to forgive and comfort him, so that he will not be overwhelmed by excessive sorrow. I urge you, therefore, to reaffirm your love for him.[66]

Another example of this need for mutual forgiveness and acceptance can be seen in Jesus' restoration of Peter after he had denied Him three times on the night He was arrested.[67] As we have seen, Peter repented, and Jesus restored him. However, He chose to do so publicly in front of the other disciples, making clear that they too were to accept him despite his significant sin. The apostle John chooses to record this incident in his account of the resurrection appearances of Jesus, perhaps acknowledging his acceptance of Peter's

---

63. Colossians 3:13.
64. Ephesians 4:32.
65. Romans 14:4.
66. 2 Corinthians 2:6-8.
67. John 21:15-19.

restoration for the wider church. In the book of Acts we see the other apostles and early church acknowledging Peter's primacy and leadership. Perhaps their willingness to forgive and accept Peter was strongly influenced by their awareness that they too had deserted Jesus that terrible night. Along with Peter, they had all boasted that they would never deny Him,[68] and yet they fled from Him at the very first sign of trouble.[69]

We need to ensure that we establish churches that function in practice, as well as in theory, as communities of mutual forgiveness. They need to be communities in which sin is openly acknowledged and admitted, and where its wickedness is not downplayed or trivialized. However, they need to be communities in which the grace, mercy and forgiveness of Jesus are extended to one another when there is true repentance, flowing from the realization that we are all sinners who have need of that same mercy ourselves. Only then will our churches be the 'safe spaces' that they need to be if we are to be honest about our temptations and sins. In a world that either denies the sinfulness of sin, or which demands justice without mercy to those who have fallen short, a loving community of grace and forgiveness will be a compelling demonstration of the power of the gospel. It will be a community in which we can both face the truth about our fallen flesh, and rejoice in the good news of our salvation, because our 'love covers over a multitude of sins.'[70] It will be the kind of community that people will want to join, because it is the kind of community that they know they need.

---

68. Matthew 26:35.
69. Matthew 26:56.
70. 1 Peter 4:8.

EPILOGUE:

REST AT LAST

Stand up, stand up for Jesus,
the strife will not be long;
this day the noise of battle,
the next the victor's song.
To everyone who conquers
a crown of life shall be;
we with the King of glory
shall reign eternally.
(George Duffield, 'Stand Up, Stand Up for Jesus')

On the eleventh hour, of the eleventh day, of the eleventh month of 1918 the guns finally fell silent on the Western Front. The fighting in World War I, which had lasted a gruelling four years, was finally over. Soldiers were able to put down their arms and peace returned.

Christians are involved in the fight of their lives. We face a life-long struggle against temptation and sinful desires. There is never a moment's rest from the front line. This is not a hopeless battle, because the victory has already been won for us by the Lord Jesus. We do not fight in our own strength, but rather are empowered by the Holy Spirit to put our sinful desires to death. Satan rages against us but he is a defeated enemy.

Whilst the fight can seem exhausting, and our progress to victory will be marked by failures and set-backs, it will not last forever. There will come a day when the fighting is over, and we will enter into our rest.

This day will come either when we die, and we are taken to be with the Lord to await our final resurrection to glory,[1] or when the Lord Jesus returns, and we are transformed to meet Him in the air as He brings all His glorified people with Him.[2] Sin, death and Satan will be consigned to judgement forever, never to trouble us again.[3] Our fallen flesh will be recreated to become a glorious resurrection body like that of the Lord Jesus Himself.[4] There will be no more temptation to face, whether internal or external. Our every desire will be to love, please and serve God forever. Our struggle will be over, and we will dwell in His presence in the new creation, where there will be 'no more death or mourning or crying or pain, for the old order of things has passed away.'[5] All our tears will be wiped away by God, and replaced by an eternal joy.

This vision is not just wishful thinking, but a sure and certain hope secured by the resurrection of the Lord Jesus from the dead. His disciples were eye witnesses of the glory to come.[6]

---

1. Philippians 1:23.
2. 1 Corinthians 15:51; 1 Thessalonians 4:17.
3. Revelation 20:7-10, 14.
4. 1 Corinthians 15:42-49.
5. Revelation 21:4.
6. John 1:14; 1 Corinthians 15:3-7; 2 Peter 1:16-18.

This vision is meant to sustain us in the fight. The power of the age to come has broken in to the present age because we have been united with Christ and enjoy the blessing of His Holy Spirit with us. We have been forgiven our sins and experience, even now, the power to resist temptation and sin. However, our salvation is not yet complete and we long for this ultimate consummation.

The hope of the eternal glory to come encourages us to press on and keep fighting. In the light of eternity the troubles we face are 'light and momentary'.[7] We look forward to receiving the reward for enduring to the end of the battle:

> I have fought the good fight, I have finished the race, I have kept the faith. Now there is in store for me the crown of righteousness, which the Lord, the righteous Judge, will award to me on that day.[8]

This reward is not just for apparently elite Christians – whether apostles, missionaries, evangelists, church planters or pastors like Paul. It is for each and every Christian who keeps fighting and, to use another metaphor, finishes the race:

> ... and not only to me, but also to all who have longed for his appearing.[9]

Every one of us who trusts Christ, and fights the battle against temptation, has a glorious eternal reward and inheritance to look forward to. Jesus resisted the temptation not to go the way of the cross by keeping His focus on the glory and joy that would follow His obedience. To persevere in our battle with temptation we need to look to Him and do the same:

---

7. 2 Corinthians 4:17.
8. 2 Timothy 4:7-8.
9. 2 Timothy 4:8.

And let us run with perseverance the race marked out for us, fixing our eyes on Jesus, the pioneer and perfecter of faith. For the joy that was set before him he endured the cross, scorning its shame, and sat down at the right hand of the throne of God. Consider him who endured such opposition from sinners, so that you will not grow weary and lose heart.[10]

As Christians we find ourselves in the 'fight of our lives'. It is not the 'fight *for* our lives' because Jesus has already saved us, and we have entered eternal life already and have passed from death to life.[11] It is not a fight that will last forever, because a day will come when our life appears:

When Christ, who is your life, appears, then you also will appear with him in glory.[12]

Until that glorious day we must keep fighting, trusting in the power of the death and resurrection to resist temptation, and relying on the work of the Holy Spirit who is dwelling within us.

Finish then your new creation,
pure and sinless let us be;
let us see your great salvation
perfect in eternity:
changed from glory into glory
till in heaven we take our place,
till we lay our crowns before you,
lost in wonder, love and praise.
(Charles Wesley, 'Love Divine All Loves Excelling')

---

10. Hebrews 12:1-3.
11. 1 John 3:14.
12. Colossians 3:4.